MY RECYCLED PETS
Diary of a Dog Addict

Randi Berger

 BOOK PUBLISHERS NETWORK

Book Publishers Network
P.O. Box 2256
Bothell • WA • 98041
Pн • 425-483-3040

10 9 8 7 6 5 4 3 2

Printed in the United States of America

LCCN: 2007932341
ISBN10: 1-887542-52-3
ISBN13: 978-1-887542-52-4

Editor/Proofreader: Julie Scandora
Cover Design: Laura Zugzda
Interior Layout: Stephanie Martindale
Front cover photo credit: Rebecca Murray, Invisible Fence Northwest
Back cover photo credit: RaeZimmermanPhotos.com

Thank you God for giving me the sense to stay out of your way and the courage to follow your lead, allowing you to miraculously supply enough and more for me to live beyond my wildest dreams. This is your will for us all.

DEDICATION

This is dedicated to the person who showed me how to love unconditionally what some people considered to be the undesirables.
For this, your superhuman patience in raising me and your constant encouragement that has steered so very many humans away from
conforming against their hearts' desires, I thank you, Mom. You are one
of the world's greatest animal lovers and saints!

CONTENTS

ACKNOWLEDGEMENTS

Some of you I speak to often. Some of you I haven't spoken to in quite some time. Some of you I have never spoken to. And some of you have transcended. But these words could not go without saying. You have all touched my life and/or the lives of my recycled pets in the most priceless of ways.

Thank you to Sarah Belgard, the silent heartbeat behind Recycled Pets who has been responsible for helping thousands of people and animals. Thank you also to Martha Burns, Barbara Miller, and Marcie Sherman, Recycled Pets' longtime, very patient, undying volunteers and friends.

The warmest of thanks also to Susie Asher; Rose and Brian Backman; Garm Beall; Michael Bell; my Berger family; Randi Besse; Beverly Oaks Animal Hospital; Linda Burgess; the Burke family; Leo Buscalgia; Annette Cenkner; Steven Colley; Mel Collins; Karen Connell and Lynn Fergesen; James Craig, DVM; Ann Cruchley; Ram Dass; Ray Dixon and Alex Marshall; Ryan Dolan; Elger Bay Grocery and Gifts; Dennis Fromin; Dee Garden; Mark Gates; Larry Golden at the Medicine Shoppe; my adopted husband and wife, Mitch and Barbara Gordon; Ed and

Norma Gordon; Mary Jo and Hank Greenberg Foundation; Jill Haber; Perry Haberman; Sheryn Hara; Brian Heimer, DVM; Tanis Helliwell; James Herriot; Alan Immerman; Glen Jacobson; DeEtte Kearns; Thomas Kinkade; Mike Klein at the Stanwood Wells Fargo; Gary and Judy Kornfein; Tina Ladd; Rich Mack; Macy's of Burlington, Washington; Jo and John Magistad; Steven Manning; Peter and Laurie Marshall; Rochelle Vestal-Maxheimer; Susan McCoy; Damon and Mike at Mike the Printer; Marsha Miller; Candy Monteiro; Roger Moss; Rebecca Murray; Craig and Joy Nadel; Dr. Pankaj Naram; Ginger Navarro; Nikken and many of its magnificent messengers; Moira O'Heren, Harold Cox and family; Peggy Paddock; Joelle Paganucci; Pet Assistance; Lori Golden at the Pet Press; Julie Prem; Mel Richkind, DVM; David Roe, the proud founder of Pacific Coast Dog Rescue; Susan Rios; Bob Ross; Craig Samuelson; Lisa Saxton; Dan Schaller; Benno Sebastian; Seflin Investigations, Inc.; Edward M. Sherman, Esq.; Jim Shipley; Florence Scovel Shinn; Mary Beth and Michael Speer; Tarzana Pet Clinic; Bruno Uptagrafft; Irma Vazquez; Jerry Wall at The Center for Natural Knowing; Neale Donald Walsch; Tammie Watters; Debbie Weiseman; Sandi Wirth; Margot Wood; World Ministry of Prayer; Patrick and Michael Wright; Ray Wurfl; and Carol Zender.

To my heaven-sent typist, Rebekah Berger: In my unwillingness to learn to type or use a computer, I picked you out of the phone book only because of your name. As busy as you told me you were, I thank you for making time for me and patiently being at my beck and call since that conversation in 2002. You have been an irreplaceably stable force in my life!

Much of this book was written to the healing, soothing, and unearthly music of Tim Janis. T.J., you remain my greatest inspiration, setting the highest example on how to focus on our purpose here. Your music brought words out of me that I was unaware existed. I thank you for creating beyond the limits of the human mind and having the courage to share your magic with the world.

The biggest thank you to Samantha Lewis. Over the years, you taught me how to focus on what I wanted to create and then helped me to manifest it. What a blessed, limitless creation my life has been because of you!

Tobi Knight, thank you for appearing at the most transitional time of my life and bringing Nam-myoho-renge-kyo to me.

Al and Winnie Emerson, I know you are still here. Thank you for safely bringing us to your home and continuing to watch over your island.

Laila del Monte, Jerry Wall, and the many healers who have most recently come into my life. You have helped me prove that thoughts and energy often have far more power than conventional medicine. Thank you for helping me to remove early death sentences that were placed on our superior four-legged ones.

Jay Goodwin of Smokey Point Chiropractic: I believe that Skooter's last resurrection was partially due to the Spinal Network Care that you had just started with both of us. Your powerful energy and work surpasses anything I've ever known and has shifted my life forever.

For the hundreds of you I may have forgotten, forgive me. My brain sometimes travels to places far beyond, leaving behind my heart's mind.

And finally, thanks to the thousands of you who have adopted or loved one of my recycled pets. You have made our world a better place.

CHAPTER 1

HOW IT ALL BEGAN

The veterinary technician from a Southern California animal shelter held the needle, about to euthanize an unwanted dog. Suddenly, he stopped himself and phoned me. "Randi, I'm looking into the eyes of this little guy, and I just can't bring myself to do it."

Jeff and I had been helping each other for quite some time now. Knowing I would always rescue the homely or elderly dog, he felt safe in phoning me at 11 p.m. to do so.

"Is he over ten years old?" I suspiciously asked. In my five years of rescuing hundreds of dogs, I was familiar with the fibbing that often goes with coercing people to take the very old and unadoptable ones.

"No, but he's pretty pathetic looking and a bit sheepish now that he's sick. He's a perfect Randi dog. You'll love him!"

"I'll be there in the morning," I said, with hesitancy in my voice.

I once heard a doctor say that alarm clocks were hazardous to the health of humans. I agreed. I had already spent my short life seemingly in opposition with what the rest of the world believed *should* be done.

This, however, was the one instance in which I would conform. I set my dusty alarm clock to 7 a.m., accepting that this would be yet another one of my many sleepless nights.

The nighttime hours have always been very holy and magical to me. This is when most humans are tucked into bed and those who are open to the creative flow of the universe could celebrate those gifts that clearly came to them from places far beyond. My nights are spent either playing the flute or writing, intertwined with nurturing the many dogs who share my space. My concept of time has always been quite skewed, and I love losing myself in it.

I did make a half-hearted attempt to force myself to sleep some time after 3 a.m., but my active mind kept me awake. What happens if I don't connect with this dog? Will Jeff forgive me if I don't take this dog whose life he spared? How many other dogs will I want to rescue from this shelter? How many of them will be sick, as so many are in the shelters? My over-active mind began twirling so fast that I couldn't keep up with it. It catapulted me thirty years back to how all of this began.

Burbank, California: 1962

I can almost remember screaming at the doctors and nurses of St. Joseph's Hospital who delivered me: "What? Are you all novices, or is it lack of sleep that makes you so incompetent?" Actually, mine was a normal delivery, and I weighed in at seven pounds, eleven ounces. My father, Richard Berger, was an art director, and my mother, Marcia Sherman, was a housewife-turned-attorney after they separated and divorced when I was fourteen years old. I was the youngest of three kids with a protective, athletic brother, Fred, six years older than I am, and a sister, Julie, eighteen months my senior, a butterfly trapped in a human package, wearing red ringlets for hair.

My handsome father, who resembled Kirk Douglas, was short on words but blatantly direct and occasionally offensive to those with whom he lost his patience—and that included almost everyone. He pulled no punches, and I praised him for it, realizing I too would be blessed with these traits, or so I thought a blessing it would be.

My mother, whom people often mistook as Lucille Ball, was the antithesis of my father. Her reality was of fairy tales, magic, and white chariots gliding out of the sky to take us on wild fantasies. I hoped to be like her but more often found myself stuck in the dreary reality of our planet.

By the age of two, I can recall arguing in full sentences with my saint-like grandmother, Lil Sherman, while she was babysitting the three of us. "You are bad cook. I not eat this food! It is bad!" For years, our family gathering conversations included my grandmother laughing so profusely she would almost wet her pants while reminiscing, "I can't believe I actually fought with a two-year-old. The worst part was she always won these battles."

By the age of four, I had already begun my own acting and law careers, speaking with a Southern drawl and threatening anyone who stepped onto *my* property: "Get out of here or I'll sue you for trespassin'!" Apparently, I was born fighting for what I perceived to be justice.

I had an intense bond with my mother. Those who knew us feared that the umbilical cord had never really been cut. She was not allowed to talk on the phone, enter the bathroom, or leave the house without my imp-like silhouette attached to her legs.

I spent much of my time watching my mother sleep, fearing she would not return. In an effort to wake her one afternoon, when I was five and she was taking a much-deserved nap, I climbed up on the kitchen counter and attempted to overdose on Chalks candy-like children's vitamins. The only one who found this performance to be entertaining was I.

I dreaded leaving my mother to begin school. I remember the dramatic scene I caused, clutching onto her legs like a locust and screaming in horror as she attempted to leave me behind. The thought of being forced to spend hours shut in a room with other humans my age, listening to the drone of some boring adult, was something that absolutely made no sense to me. When I finally succumbed, I was more interested in counting the squares on the ceiling and analyzing why this boring adult picked out the clothes that she'd chosen to wear each day than in listening to the meaningless drivel she was uttering.

It seems that I fought every step of life, from the imperfect lumps in my thick waist-length red braids that my tolerant mother spent hours redoing every morning upon my demand to the grotesque thoughts of eating with silverware that human mouths other than my own may have touched. Oh yes, I temper-tantrumed my way to manipulating my mother into carrying plastic dinnerware with her at all times or I would not dine in any restaurants. Then, I would order the most expensive item on the menu—usually filet mignon—and not eat it.

In retrospect, I am aware that had I been born to any other mother, the rest of my life would have been spent being bounced around from foster home to foster home.

My neuroses carried over into my discerning preferences with my couture. Although barely in grade school, I had already made it a habit to change my clothes at least three times before reaching my own final verdict. No pair of socks would remain on my feet if one thread could be felt by my oversensitive epidermis.

My carefree sister, Julie, as opposite from me as a sister could be, was content simply wearing her flowered flannel pajama bottoms to school. Absentmindedly, she had done this several times with no shame. But my fastidiousness was now detrimentally affecting Julie's grades. Her teacher informed her that she could not have any more tardies or her perfect report card would be tarnished. This did not concern me in the least.

"Teachers can't boss us around" I yelled at my mother and sister one morning, on my fifth change of clothes and still not satisfied.

My mother calmly pleaded with me, "Randi, this is not fair to Julie. Either you get in the car now, or we're leaving without you."

I screamed back, "I'm not ready. Then go without me. I don't care!"

When my overly patient mother's hands gently slipped around my neck and would not release, I actually thought to myself, "Wow! Now she deserves some respect! She should have done this years earlier."

For reasons unknown to my family, I made friends quite easily. I discarded them just as easily. I had little interest in spending much time with kids my own age. Nonetheless, it seemed I had gained control over all of the neighborhood kids and elected myself as the ringleader who would keep our territory in order. I would decide which child in our neighborhood should be tormented at any given time, and the rest of the pack would carry out my strategic, evil plans. Even my sweet sister Julie followed my lead.

My family celebrated my seventh birthday at an animal shelter, where I picked out my first very own puppy to be a companion to our existing dog, Skippy. Skippy was a scruffy, tan, midsize terrier mix, who spent the first year of his life living in our backyard as an only dog. He was the sort of dog with whom every child dreams of sharing magical moments. But Julie had picked out Skippy for her seventh birthday. Now, it was my turn.

All five of us piled into our boat-size Chevy Caprice, with my brother and me kicking at each other in the backseat. As usual, my butterfly-like sister was daydreaming out the window and peacefully bird-watching in her own private world.

As the five of us stumbled into the shelter, my brother stepped on the back of my shoe in hopes of rejoicing over my falling on my face as my special birthday gift from him. I kicked him in the shin while I excitedly clutched my mother's and father's hands, forcefully swinging their arms back and forth almost in full circle. Secretly, I knew that I was both my parents' favorite child.

Most of the everyday stuff of life bored me so, and I thought that every day should be my birthday. This was the most exciting adventure in my entire life. Dogs everywhere—young and old, rat-size to elephant-size, solid color to polka-dot—and they all had so many interesting things to say to me.

Wide-eyed, with an ear-to-ear grin and full of focus like never before in my life, I squealed, "I want them all," while tugging at my dad's arm.

"No, Randi. You can pick one," my dad replied, surveying all of the wagging tails through the cage bars.

"But I love all of them! We could get a bigger house. I can quit school and stay home to take care of them," I whined back to uninterested ears.

It was no surprise that we went home with a scruffy, tan, over-grown, little boy terrier puppy who looked just like Skippy. This puppy had it made because he was mine. I named him Lucky, believing that he would forever bring me good fortune.

Lucky and Skippy became my everything, although they were forced to live as outside dogs. Even then, I knew that we were the worst dog owners in the world, and I pleaded with my parents, "Can't they just come in at night? I'll train them."

He's not heavy, he's my new dog, Lucky!

As usual, the word "no" was not a part of my ears' recognizable vocabulary, and I snuck them inside to the opposite end of the house from where the bedrooms were, praying that they would not make a noise. Unfortunately, the dogs used the door moldings and our set of Britannica encyclopedias as chew toys that first night, which marked the end of their brief experience as indoor dogs.

I was angry at Julie for not fighting alongside me for the rights of Lucky and Skippy. But her head was off in the clouds somewhere, so I had to retaliate. One rainy night, while I began to sink into a mild depression thinking about "my boys" in the cold and darkness of their doghouse, some brilliant and uplifting ideas came to me. The next morning, I awoke in a very chipper mood as I watched Julie roll over on a pillow full of slugs that "mysteriously" had crept into her bed. The rest of my family would enjoy a delightful breakfast of Cheerios laced with salt that had been "mysteriously" placed in the sugar container.

I went from childhood to adolescence preferring to carry on my conversations with Lucky and Skippy instead of my family or peers. It seemed that no one understood me as well as they did, and I certainly couldn't understand the thought processes of most humans—nor did I want to. I was more than content, and quite proud to admit, that my best friends did indeed have four legs.

There are some other unmentionables that I now must mention about my family during my grade school years. Anyone looking at us through a spy-scope lens would either be much entertained or wonder why we weren't in group therapy.

My mother, in the midst of her fantasies, became very involved with our drama department at Encino Elementary School and began writing and directing our plays. She clearly thought it was normal to drive her children to and from school wearing a Bozo the Clown costume. I was coerced into playing the pig in *Alice in Blunderland*, and hence, my nickname for the remainder of my grade school years—Piggy.

Thank God, I was born with an overly strong sense of self. A "normal" child would probably have developed some sort of a complex. But not me. I began collecting everything that had to do with pigs and never again ate pork. Just the mere thought of it became cannibalistic to me.

At the same time I fell in love with pigs, Julie fell in love with goats. Lucky and Skippy were given a new sibling, a little girl Nubian goat named Nanny. Living in a non-agricultural, proper, suburban area, we hoped that our neighbors would believe that the loud "naaa-ing" coming from our backyard was simply a new dog with an unusual voice. But Nanny was not content with canine brothers. When her unique "barking" frequented the majority of the nighttime hours, my mom's true love of animals began to emerge, and she retired each night to our backyard with a sleeping bag next to Nanny so that she would not be lonely.

We became the talk of Encino, and people flocked to our house to meet Nanny. But a sourpuss living in the neighborhood rained on our parade and complained. Julie cried during the entire ride back to Nanny's original home when we were forced to reunite her with her family.

Just before entering junior high, Julie and I had become close friends with Elizabeth McGovern and her younger sister Cami. My mom had corrupted shy Liz into performing in her plays at Encino Elementary School. The rest is history.

Liz and Cami were some of the first humans I felt almost as close to as my dogs. They were both genuine, empathetic animal and nature lovers. Liz instantly felt like a protective big sister and seemed much nicer than Julie.

The four of us would escape into the lush, tree-laden hills of Encino that included sacred Indian burial grounds. Our imaginations took us to grand, faraway places where unicorns, fairies, and wizards greeted us and invited us to stay forever. Forever was never long enough.

One rainy winter day, not the sort of day the four of us could escape to explore more of life on the other side, we were all at Liz's house. She was playing her new flute. Truthfully, to me it seemed more as if she was *attempting* to play it; she sounded more like a duck crying out for help. Liz passed around the flute for all of us to try, and before it was even my turn, I started to say, "I can't. I can't." I had already developed a habit of using those words before trying something new. I was born with the belief that if I couldn't be the best at something, why even try?

"Just place the mouthpiece under your lower lip, gently purse your mouth, and release a small stream of air into the opening," Liz said encouragingly.

I think I was more stunned than anyone else when the tone that came out was full, clear, and sounded, at least to me, like a wondrous addition to a world-class symphony. That moment began the next phase of my life, and through much of junior high and high school, I found myself sitting first-chair flute. We all suggested that Liz stick with acting.

By this time, I had become more open to having some human friends in my life. Julie had given her wholehearted attempt at playing the oboe, and our house was filled with other musicians, private flute and oboe tutors, and our duets for the next five years. Occasionally, we would hear Lucky and Skippy attempting to serenade us from the backyard. I was now preoccupied with being the best flutist in my junior high and high school. I practiced up to eight hours a day to ensure my success. There was no time for dogs.

I creatively figured out ways to avoid most of my other classes as they so bored me. I spent the majority of seventh through twelfth grades playing my flute and causing trouble in the music department. Those who were subjected to my presence all fell victim to my continuing mischievous pranks.

I still wore long red braids in junior high and I loved tormenting Mrs. Brown, our music teacher. Mrs. Brown was a robust, determined woman, who conducted with a fierce seriousness. But I was even more determined than she. I was on a mission to lighten her up.

One day I went to school wearing wires throughout my long, red braids in Pippi Longstocking mode. While we were in deep concentration, performing *Pomp and Circumstance* to Mrs. Brown's serious conducting, I bent my braids up in the air during a brief period when the flutes were not playing. While at rest, I slipped my flute through my braids where it sat suspended in air until she caught sight of it. When Mrs. Brown gasped and dropped her baton, the music abruptly stopped. The sudden silence seemed even louder than the music that I had just extinguished. I was sure that that day would be the end of my music career, but it was not, and the fun continued.

Mrs. Brown eventually did lighten up, and she became more of a friend than a teacher. Many of us grew so attached to her that we dreaded leaving junior high and moving on to high school.

Next to be subjected to my rebelliousness was old Mr. Wurfl. Mr. Wurfl was in charge of the music department at Birmingham High School, and he was probably the first disciplinarian I ever encountered. But I grew on him too. He challenged my musical abilities, inspiring me also to learn to play the saxophone so that I could be in all of his classes.

Mr. Wurfl had a fan club of those who understood him, but to some, he could be quite intimidating. I looked at his personality as a challenge, and I was compelled to discover what was underneath his stoic nature. Besides, how could anyone be intimidated by someone who wore a toupee and conducted our marching band with such ferociousness that the glue would drip down his forehead? The toupee was no secret to any of us, but Mr. Wurfl still demanded respect, and he got it, even from me.

Mr. Wurfl's breaking point was when I showed up late to one of our Friday night football games mildly intoxicated and rolled down the bleachers. Again, playing first chair flute and now also piccolo, this was not setting a very good example to the others. With steam coming out of his ears, Mr. Wurfl grabbed me and all but dragged me out of view from the hundreds of observers in the stands.

"Randi! You're not to leave tonight without talking to me. Meet me in the music room after the game." I was truly frightened, realizing that this time I might have rocked the boat (or the bleachers) a little too far. I was sure I would at least be suspended from school.

"Randi, what the hell do you think you were doing out there?" Mr. Wurfl scolded me in his most stern voice ever.

In a manipulative, coy way, I sweetly replied, "I was so nervous to perform tonight. I didn't want to come at all. Instead of not showing up, I came … well, I came a little relaxed. I didn't realize how sensitive I was to vodka."

Mr. Wurfl was far too insightful to believe me, but he did a wonderful job of pretending, and I too played dumb, an ability that kept me away from disciplinary actions throughout my high school days.

Mr. Wurfl and I grew to understand and appreciate one another, and after my drunken stupor escapade, he offered to drive me home from school anytime I ever wanted his company. After that night, Mr. Wurfl overlooked most of the marching band getting drunk on our bus rides to football games at other high schools. He was retiring soon and seemed to become more like one of us than the authoritarian we had all once feared.

I didn't know what I would do without Mr. Wurfl. I celebrated his farewell football game with one of my best friends, Leah Marderosian, who also played the flute. We supplied our marching band with Ex-Lax chocolate chip cookies that we baked for the occasion. I apologize to any of you who missed school the next day.

When Mr. Wurfl retired, almost at the same time that Julie left forever to go away to college at Humboldt University, I think I did everything within my power to hide my truth. I was finally becoming attached to humans.

One early morning before the sun had risen, I remember swallowing my pain.

"Good-bye, Randi, my baby sister. I'm leaving for college," Julie whispered in my ear.

I pretended to sleep through Julie's last kiss good-bye, but everyone knew that I never slept that deeply. I didn't want her to know that, underneath my unyielding shell, I would feel lost without her.

With Julie's absence and Mr. Wurfl's retirement, playing my flute never quite held the same meaning for me.

Skippy and Lucky were now eleven and ten years old and had become nothing more than a significant part of our backyard décor. My memories of them during junior high and high school were of merely dumping a can of food into each of their bowls and quickly giving them a dinnertime hug. Never again would the three of us share those wondrous afternoons filled with endless searches for four-leaf clovers. I had all but forgotten about our surreal evenings that were once graced by the many wishes we had made together on shooting stars. Adolescence had stolen my boys away from me.

The following year, when Lucky was only eleven, I was calling him for dinner one evening, and my heart sank. Lucky always immediately came bounding up to me, but that night he was nowhere in sight.

"Lucky, my baby! Where are you?" I frantically yelled. I searched our backyard with my heart racing. When I found him in a remote spot in the yard asleep, I jumped away screaming. I ran off in horror when I realized that this sleep was never-ending. My good luck charm, my seventh birthday present who was once my everything had died of a heart attack.

I thought Skippy and I would never recover from Lucky leaving us so abruptly. My insides ached even more when Skippy's grief seemed to surpass my own. He stopped eating and would howl during the nights in hopes of calling Lucky back to him so that they could finish their lives here together.

I remember begging Julie to come back from Humboldt College as I hysterically sobbed to Tom Petty, singing on the radio, "The waiting is the hardest part." That song will always remind me of my first experience with death and the realization that some things in life I could not control.

Brokenhearted and with no clear direction as to what path I would follow after high school, I did what everyone else was doing and took the Scholastic Aptitude Test to enter college. I truly had no desire to go to college and be trapped for more years by society's attempts at brainwashing, but when I scored below average on the SAT because I left in the midst of the exam due to boredom, I once again had to fight back. I wrote an essay that resulted in the president of California State University, Northridge, graciously opening his arms to me. Before I could even figure out what I was doing in college, I found myself majoring in psychology and theater. Most of the classes were utterly dull to me, and I struggled through college, always searching for any unique, unconventional class that would count toward my major. How I received a bachelor's degree with classes such as Interpersonal Communication and Group Dynamics, Psychodrama, and Weekend Encounter Groups, which gave me credit for an entire semester, was beyond me. I believe I was the only person ever to graduate from CSUN without taking a foreign language or any math.

I spent most of these college years dodging male suitors. I was as disinterested in relationships, marriage, and bearing children as I had been with kids my own age when I was a child. People often questioned whether or not I was interested in the opposite gender, but the truth was that most humans rarely stimulated my psyche enough for me to desire spending much time with anyone. I always preferred my own company to anyone else's. It had nothing to do with gender.

It took an intense, spiritual, charming, gregarious, tall, successful Italian salesman ten years my senior to turn my head. Before I knew it, I was engaged to Dan Schaller at the young age of twenty. We celebrated a spontaneous, enlightening, and passionate courtship, and I slowly began moving my things into his place.

But by my twenty-first birthday, I realized that continuing this union would be the end of me. Dan wanted a wife to bear his children, someone he could protect, watch over, and worship twenty-four hours a day, seven days a week. I was accustomed to meandering through my life, in control and unattended. Our differences were becoming volcanic, and I walked away from a marriage, a house in Malibu, and a promised Porsche to match his own Porsche. I felt empowered at the age of twenty-one as I discovered those things I would treasure always—my freedom, independence, and peaceful solitude would never be traded for anyone at anytime or for any price.

With some time apart, Dan and I resurrected our friendship and continued to honor those priceless lessons we both learned from each other.

Skippy was now fourteen and, out of the blue, disappeared from my mother's backyard. Our gardeners had come and gone, inadvertently leaving our gate open.

The following week we received a letter from the Department of Animal Regulations with these words: "We are sorry to inform you that your dog has been injured. Please contact us immediately."

When I returned to the shelter where, fourteen years earlier, we had carried out Skippy as our new puppy only to see him now crippled, I was unable to control my tears. I realized that the second half of his life had been spent devoid of my affection. I was unaware that so much time had passed, and that his vision was almost nonexistent. He didn't recognize me until I spoke to him, "Skippy, my beautiful, handsome boy. I miss you so much." Although he was unable to move, his tail and bladder were still working. An enormously dry lump in my throat caused me to choke when Skippy began to urinate on himself with his tail thumping against the back of the small cage where he had been isolated. How could he even remember a voice he had barely heard in nine years, and more important, why would he forgive me?

Skippy had been hit by a car and now had seven fractures in his pelvis.

Dan was very supportive and drove us through the San Fernando Valley searching for a vet who would see Skippy without an appointment on a Saturday. We were losing hope as every vet turned us away. We finally found someone, Dr. Deborah Hoffman, who had recently opened her practice and who greeted us with a very encouraging smile. Although she could barely maneuver herself around the examining table due to being eight months pregnant, Dr. Hoffman was someone I knew from that moment that I would want to keep in my life. The vets who didn't have the time to see Skippy all said things such as "He's fourteen. He's had a good life. I'm a little busy now so why don't you bring him back Monday and we can put him to sleep for you" or "There is no likelihood of a dog this age recovering from such severe trauma." But Dr. Hoffman had the optimistic attitude that I had grown to adore from my mother. "These types of injuries usually heal on their own. We can give him some painkillers and let him have the rest he needs to recover. He'll probably be fine in a month or so."

I was in love with Dr. Hoffman.

At the age of fourteen, Skippy began living the life he had always deserved. He became our beloved and cherished *indoor bed dog*. In no time at all, Skippy completely healed and once again became our puppy. My mom and I spent every waking moment idolizing his every move, breath, blink, yawn, grunt, and smell and fighting over his delicious geriatric kisses. Our backyard was now only used as his bathroom, and Skippy would never again feel the loneliness he suffered when he lost his brother years earlier.

Even after graduating from college, I had recurring nightmares about my car breaking down, causing me to miss my last final exam. In my nightmares, I was the only person in the world with a phantom diploma. I presume my subconscious was not feeling very scholarly and that I truly deserved a bachelor's degree. However, a bachelor's degree in psychology and theater was basically useless. I contemplated more routine jail time by attending Pepperdine University in Malibu, which would result in some impressive initials after my name. But instead, I opted to stay more within my comfort zone and began taking classes at the Lee Strasberg Theatre Institute in West Hollywood, where I thought I would have more freedom. I was wrong and was soon to be near death from boredom.

One of my first classes was filled with over twenty starry-eyed, struggling actors. By the end of the term, there were three people left in the class: two men in their twenties and me.

We spent most of the semester sitting in our chairs in a circle caressing a hot cup of coffee that did not exist. The best part was having our instructor, who looked like Paul Newman, screaming at us with veins popping out of his neck, "Damn it! Your jaw is not relaxed. I can see tension in your right foot!" as he kicked at the foot of the girl across from me. "You will never make it as an actress!" This girl did not take his "instruction" well and ran out of the room crying, never to return.

My classmates, both men and women, were dropping out like flies. I finished that class only to prove that my will was stronger than that of this instructor.

My favorite memory from the Strasberg institute took place in the auditorium where we were attending a seminar led by the country's top instructors. Students eagerly volunteered to go on stage and be critiqued by these "stars." Comments from the audience were encouraged. Although I never raised my hand to participate in any of this, I was asked to give my opinion of the student who had just exited the stage crying. She was unable to move or speak when she walked on stage, and she was one of the more advanced students.

I wanted to slide off my chair and disappear, but as the hundred-plus people in the audience were staring at me, waiting for my critique, I was forced to speak my truth. "Honestly, it seems that she needs therapy to help her overcome her stage fright."

I envisioned the tomatoes coming at me as I was verbally chastised by one of the top instructors: "You clearly know nothing about method acting."

"If that was method acting," I said only to myself, "then I hope I never do understand it."

One of my instructors, whom I actually thought was quite delightful and whose classes I enjoyed, pulled me aside after the seminar.

"Randi, the monologues you've been writing are just wonderful. You really should consider writing instead of acting," she diplomatically soothed me.

"If they didn't want the truth, they shouldn't have asked my opinion. I'm sorry. I wasn't impressed with any of this," I calmly replied.

I suppose it would have sounded prestigious to be able to say I graduated from the Lee Strasberg Theatre Institute, but method acting and lying to myself about enjoying this ride was one performance I was unwilling to continue.

As Dan, college, and the Strasberg institute drifted into my past, a new love drifted into my present—body building.

I became so completely entranced with perfecting my package to my critical standards that I would set my alarm clock to 3 a.m. to go work out in an uncrowded twenty-four-hour gym. I preferred working out alone, when the many fitness club socialites were in deep slumber. These are the people who pretend to work out when, in fact, they are just lonely and bored. Those types of people certainly would not be at a gym at 3:30 a.m. when there was no one to bother except for me.

It was when I joined Gold's Gym that I discovered how much my mind could control my body. At only five feet, two inches tall, I would say to myself, while leg-pressing over four hundred, "I am easily and effortlessly pushing only air. This air feels very, very light to me," and so on.

Men would gawk in disbelief as I leg-pressed hundreds of pounds more than some of them did on a good day. I refrained from speaking my thoughts: "If I sat around like you, watching other people work out, I too would be weak."

Through the pungent smell of musky sweat and the loud clanking of heavy weights, I often heard people ask, "Are you a professional body builder? How long have you been competing?" I would politely smile back while counting my repetitions and thinking, "Why don't you stop watching me and go get to work?"

My only competition was with myself, and I became addicted, both mentally and physically, to this empowering sport. I went to the gym for one purpose only and immediately left when finished. Socializing was not on my agenda, and I always rushed home to rendezvous with my Skippy, who never failed to be leaning against the front door, awaiting my return. Nothing was more exciting to me than a late Saturday night workout at an empty Gold's Gym and rekindling my lost love with Skippy. All of my childhood anger was being released by pushing dumbbells and heavy iron plates that to me were simply air.

On March 17, 1987, this cruel world decided Skippy's time was up. Although he was seventeen, it seemed far too soon for us. I wanted to believe my mom: "Death only exists for those who accept it." But cancer had spread throughout Skippy's nose. The epinephrine we were squirting in his nostrils to stop his bloody sneezing attacks was no longer working. He was now having grand mal seizures.

I drowned my anger in my weight lifting while my mom went into denial and could not talk about Skippy's condition. It felt as if we had been bothering Dr. Hoffman every day, but as usual, she was extraordinarily patient and encouraging. A part of me hoped that the white chariot would come out of the sky to take Skippy. My mom never lost her dreams and fantasies over the years and promised me that this was how Skippy would leave. I so wanted to believe her. I was angry that I was not given the powers to heal animals.

When Skippy finally went into a coma, I was calmer than I would have expected. My mom, however, was not. I carried Skippy's limp body into Dr. Hoffman's office, still hoping for that miracle. My mom came shortly afterward, but could not bring herself to look at Skippy when she knew he was never coming home.

As we aimlessly walked out to our cars in the dark alley behind Dr. Hoffman's office, I felt I had taken on Skippy's coma. My car would not start, so I left it in the parking lot. I just did not have the strength to cope with any more problems. I drove home with my mom, both of us staring ahead in complete silence.

When we walked through our front door where Skippy was usually pressed, we were met with a dark eeriness in the house that we had never before felt. All of the power and electricity had vanished, exactly as it had with my car. There was no earthly, logical explanation for any of this, but neither of us was in a mood to analyze it.

March 17, 1987, St. Patrick's Day, was the darkest day I had ever known.

Life as I knew it came to a halt. I spent weeks by my mom's side, both of us feeling as though our five senses had been stripped from us. I couldn't live with the pain of staying in a home where I watched Skippy's soul slip away from me. Julie came home for the summer, and the two of us spent the next few months traveling through the United States with a group of her friends while I searched for some answers.

We ended up at a Grateful Dead show in Berkeley, California. The sixties had returned, and the splendor of seeing people laughing while dancing in the streets, wearing brightly colored tie-dyed clothing, seemed to be a suitable panacea for my sorrow. Even the dogs were dressed in matching tie-dyes, and I was in awe over every four-legged glow who crossed my path. The sweet wafting of marijuana, which seemed to be a constant aroma at the Grateful Dead show, had no appeal to me compared with throwing my arms around any dog who would not run from my overly enthusiastic advances. I glanced over my shoulder to a stranger sitting next to me on a curb and was amazed at how highly skilled he was in the intricate task of rolling marijuana cigarettes with no fear of being arrested. I looked up to a screaming crowd that had parted to make way for a twenty-foot-tall Grim Reaper walking on stilts, waving to his fans. This felt like home, and I hoped never to return to the bleak reality of a world that had stolen my greatest love from me.

But I was jolted out of this fantasy when I heard the screeching of car tires and a dog yelping in pain. My jovial mood disappeared and I flashed back to Skippy being hit by the car three years earlier. I began to sob and Julie grabbed me, hugging me tightly. At that moment, I was driven to return home.

Slowly, hesitantly, I began to frequent the animal shelters and adoption facilities in the San Fernando Valley. After learning the tragic and unjust statistics of animals unnecessarily euthanized daily, I began to see that there was a definite reason I experienced the void and pain I did from Skippy's death. All of my tenacity, independence, and strength would now be used to begin the greatest mission my life would ever know.

Today, twenty years later, I have rescued, rehabilitated, and found homes for thousands of dogs through my dog rescue agency, Recycled Pets. The bachelor's degree I had received in psychology and theater was used to counsel people needing to place their dogs, people grieving the loss of their dogs, people coming to me to adopt a dog, and the many abused and neglected dogs that soon filled my life.

I would be one of the first people in Southern California to hold exciting open-house dog adoption events at locations such as pet shops, parks, and coffeehouse patios. Hordes of eager people would arrive early to adopt dogs from my rescue agency. This was when I learned the skill of matching humans with their new canine counterparts. My dog rescue agency would also become the vehicle where I would be joined with many of my lifelong friends.

I always have written about my rescues, amounting to more than twenty journals. Some of my rescues have impacted me in heart-wrenching ways, some contain astonishing synchronicities, and some have been nothing short of incomprehensible miracles. These are the stories my soul poured onto paper with ease, creating an insightful haven for the human spirit.

On my thirty-ninth birthday, I made a commitment to myself to finally turn my most memorable stories into a book that would infuse readers with the hope of self-help, the comfort of spirituality, and the realization that even the impossible dares to be possible. The following evening, I sat outside until sunrise, releasing the most intense tears I had ever known for no reason of which I was consciously aware. That next morning, September 11, 2001, my commitment to finish this book exploded into a vow.

And so, I am grateful that most of my life has been filled with the passion of rescuing and helping these superior, four-legged life forms. And I am even more grateful that, since 1987, I ignored the numerous, unsolicited comments from family and friends urging me to do something more conventional and lucrative with my life. Although I vowed to shut down my rescue more times than I can count, this has yet to happen. The one subject that always seemed to grab people's hearts and soften the hardest of egos was dogs. Dogs are an unusually unifying force on this planet. They are the one species most trained and cherished for rescuing other lives in more ways than just physically. I was never able to turn my back on my passion for nurturing the unwanted and undesirable dogs that crossed my path.

My rescue agency also seemed to connect me with the human world, opening up complete strangers' minds to hear and trust one another. This has always been priceless to me since I've struggled with a mind that resists accepting everything as being in Divine Right Order. I continued to question my faith in people and life daily. But one July night in 2002, months after I *thought* I had finished the first edition of this book, I was driving home at around 1 a.m. with a truck full of dogs. I looked up and saw a breathtaking sky filled with soft puffy clouds. I began reciting affirmations: "My mind only knows peace. I only see life as a dream come true. I honor and cherish everyone who stands before me," and so on. Over the years, I have found affirmations like these to be the only way I could cope with life.

I had had a day of overload with too many people giving up handicapped and senior dogs, and I was frustrated, as I knew I would not be able to help them all. I was exhasted from a day of so many different life challenges being thrown at me. I was almost broken from speaking these words so many times that I again began to believe them: "I really don't need to be doing this any longer. I've been rescuing dogs fifteen years now. It's enough!"

This was also the day that I surrendered my dream of this book ever being published. I didn't have the energy to "push" it anymore. The previous week one well-respected agent informed me that he saw potential with my book but wouldn't market it unless I rewrote most of it, making it fictional. My local agent, whom I met from my rescuing, had said that she loved the book. But she hadn't replied to my last e-mail, asking her what we should do next. When she finally did reply, my heart sank. She wrote, "Randi, I'm so sorry I haven't gotten back to you. Coyotes killed two of my dogs, and it was during the day. I was there when it happened but was unable to do anything. I haven't been able to work, and I'm still numb."

I thought to myself, "How can such suffering be Divine Right Order? Why can't life ever be easy?"

But just hours before my drive home on this warm July night, I had had a conversation with one of my mentors, Samantha Lewis. Her words, once again, brought me peace. So, on this usually brief drive home from my mother's house (who assists with senior and disabled dog care), I was grateful for a detour that life put before me.

The off-ramp I always took to go home was closed. The next two off-ramps were also closed. My "normal" reaction might have been anger and impatience, but not this night. On this drive, I was deep in peaceful thoughts and aware of the beauty surrounding me. This detour I did not want to see end.

As I was driving along streets that my four-legged family and I had not previously taken this late at night, we came across something that was slowly stumbling down the middle of the street and bumping into the curbs. My patient family calmly waited in our truck and watched as I got out and approached this lost soul. As I softly began speaking to it, I realized that it could barely see or hear me. I gently began petting it and could see that it was an old, sweet, almost-blind, maybe deaf, well-groomed little boy Cocker spaniel. His name and address were illegible on his ancient, worn ID tag, but as I rubbed it, I thought I could make out the phone number. I was never so grateful for the invention of cell phones because my truck was already full of dogs and there was no way I would leave this little boy on the streets while I looked for help. I did not hesitate to wake someone up at 1 a.m. to come for a found dog. His father immediately answered the phone and was on his way. Minutes later, a tall, grandfatherly man drove up to us, leaped out of his car, and scooped up his boy, holding him in his arms like a baby.

"Me and my wife can't figure out how he got out of the house. He's never gotten out before," the man told me. "He's always with us. He's fourteen, you know."

As my eyes welled up, I replied, "I run a dog rescue agency. Would you like a new ID tag? I always carry some with me, along with leashes, collars, and usually a truck full of dogs."

I handed him a new tag along with my card, and as I drove away, higher than a kite, the memory of those big, beautiful, clouded eyes of that Cocker spaniel remained with me. Although our lives only touched for a brief moment in time, he gave me the gift of realizing that *every detour from what we think is "right" holds a message somewhere for us that EVERYTHING is always in Divine Right Order.*

Some of the true stories that these pages hold are just too amazing to be mere coincidences. I invite you to unleash your faith and your feelings while joining me through the unforgettable and often mystical journey of running my dog rescue agency, Recycled Pets.

Randi and mutts over twenty years later

CHAPTER 2

APRIL'S STORY

"Buzzzzz." Mild cardiac arrest set in as 7 a.m. approached with the brash intrusion of my ever–so dreaded alarm clock. My wandering mind disabled my body from ever going into those restful REM stages that humans need to survive. I liked to consider myself some species other than human anyway. Maybe a leprechaun. They don't require sleep either.

I found myself sitting up in bed and opened my eyes to my wonderful tribe of four-legged bedmates. I recited my morning ritual affirmations: "Today is the happiest day of my life, and again, I'm grateful for the gifts I'm about to receive and give in this day." I forced myself into making these affirmations a habit, or else I knew I could easily revert back to that wretched, angry little girl who possessed my being for the first half of my life.

In about fifteen minutes, I was out the door and amazed at how quickly I was able to exit my house now compared with my nightmarish childhood mornings. Going to school had been nothing but a tedious chore for me, but going to an animal shelter was slowly becoming an addiction. My focus and determination while driving to an animal shelter could be compared to that of an ambulance driver's. I uttered under my breath to the many dazed people on the road, obstructing traffic, "Clear the way. I have places to get to and dogs to rescue." I had yet to conquer my impatience with certain situations. Driving was one of them.

This particular animal shelter was in quite an impoverished neighborhood. I'll never forget my first visit to this facility. Graffiti decorated every sign in sight. Migrant laborers stood on street corners flagging down cars that slowly passed by in hopes of finding work for the day. Trash overflowed from the curbs up onto the sidewalks where shopping carts lay in abandonment. The front yards of homes were used as cemeteries for cars that looked as if they had died years ago.

But I was a starry-eyed, optimistic, naïve new rescuer, and my enthusiasm enabled me to ignore the burning anger and sadness I felt in the pit of my stomach as I drove through these streets and walked into this shelter.

I wanted to save all of the dogs on death row. I longed to help every dog who needed me. But this one shelter alone had hundreds of dogs needing to be rescued. Big, old, aggressive, untamed, unmaintained, and undesirable dogs filled most of the runs. Most of the smaller dogs were horribly unkempt, aged, or sickly. It could end up costing thousands of dollars just to rescue a few of these discarded beings, who apparently had never been given the opportunity to live out their roles as man's best friend.

But none of this mattered to me yet. I was a wide-eyed, bushy-tailed, passionate new rescuer, and this was a brand-new shelter to my starry eyes.

Walking through the shelter, I noticed many other human visitors grimacing while pinching their nostrils together and jamming their fingers in their ears. I was too innocent and in love with dogs to let the aroma of an understaffed, overcrowded animal shelter bother my olfactory senses. The roaring of too many unwanted pit bulls, chows, shepherds, and mongrels was new music to my ears. I was in heaven.

I stopped to talk to a cage of groveling four-legged superiors and became even more interested in a man kneeling next to me talking to what seemed to be his own pack of dogs who had been impounded. I overhead him saying, "I'm so sorry. I promise to get you guys out soon.

I'm sorry this happened to you." I could smell the faint sourness of alcohol on him. The sparkle of tears running down his face, fogging his spectacles, made me want to help this man. But out of nowhere, two police officers came up behind us and grabbed him. The man resisted, flailing his arms and trying to escape. The policemen began hitting him with their batons, and the man fell to the cement floor in a pool of drying dog urine, with his glasses shattered and blood dripping down his face.

As the alcohol-cologned man was carried away by the police officers, the music of dogs singing became still. I wondered if this man's dogs knew what had happened and if that scene traumatized them as it did me. At that moment, my innocence as a starry-eyed novice dog rescuer was demolished. The crumpled glass, blood, and urine mixed together on the hard cement floors where hundreds of unwanted dogs would temporarily reside would forever be my dark memory of this animal shelter. I hoped never to return.

But several years later, a volunteer at this same animal shelter had gotten wind of a rumor that I was successfully running my own dog adoptions at a Petco pet store in Studio City. Hundreds of dogs at this shelter were being euthanized every month, and she wanted my help in rescuing some of them before they were destroyed. When she phoned and pleaded with me, her beautiful British accent gently seduced me into a trance, and I found myself marching with my purposeful gait back into that shelter.

Jeff was the veterinary technician working there at that time, and upon meeting, we had an instant, playful bond. Jeff was almost clown-like. He had a lighthearted way about him that helped remove some of the darkness that I held within about this shelter. I sensed that Jeff was also not entirely human, which, coming from me, was a compliment.

Jeff often worked graveyard shifts at this shelter and, in addition to nurturing the sick and injured animals, had the grueling task of euthanizing those dogs whose time was up. We sort of made a nonverbal pact: he would hold certain dogs for me at the shelter and ensure that they would not be euthanized, and I would take the homely or unadoptable ones that he found himself unable to execute. To me, Jeff was close to godlike.

I met Jeff at the shelter the morning after receiving his 11 p.m. phone call. Our droopy, bloodshot eyes let each other know that neither

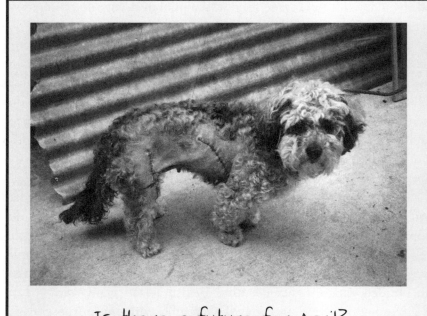

Is there a future for April?

of us had slept. But it always seemed that, upon sight of each other, we were immediately energized.

"I knew you would show up," Jeff said with his clown-like grin.

I smiled back. "You know I don't commit to something unless I'm one hundred percent sure I can. How are you doing?"

Jeff breathed a sigh of relief and said, "Good, now that you're here. I was afraid to leave this morning before you got here. They would have put this one to sleep today. Come meet him."

Jeff walked me over to the stray whose life he had spared—a mid-size male, black and white, duckfooted, shy spaniel mix with a green discharge foaming from his nose. It was only a mild upper respiratory infection, but that was a death sentence at this overcrowded shelter. I agreed to take him.

"Here," Jeff said. "I want you to continue his medications and keep him on them for another two weeks. Let me know if the infection hasn't cleared up by then."

Jeff's mouth was still moving, but his voice faded into nothingness as I began to fixate on another dog I saw in this hospital section. As Jeff was still talking to my now-deaf ears, I slowly walked away from him and approached this unwanted stray, whose red check on her kennel card meant she was on the list to be put to sleep.

I clenched my face in disbelief as I saw what appeared to be the remnant of a sweet, gentle little girl dog who was barely clinging to life. She was so mangled that it was difficult to know what breed she might be. I was so spellbound I didn't even notice that Jeff had followed me to her cage and was standing next to me.

"What happened?"

Jeff replied, sounding like a news reporter, "We don't know much about this one, but her owner has not claimed her. She's going down tonight. Someone picked her up out of the gutter after witnessing a car hit her. It dragged her for a block or so and then sped off. Probably would have been a nice little dog."

"Can I go sit with her?" I asked.

Jeff unlocked her run and let me in with her. She was unable to move. The skin along her sides was oozing and torn from road burn. She glanced up at me with a look in her eyes that told me she knew her life had no future. I knew that look well. Although I did not want to see her suffer, I felt more strongly that she now did not deserve to die. I had to help her.

Jeff had gone off to tend to the other sick and injured animals when I tracked him down and asked, "Will you release her to me? Something is telling me I have to give her a chance."

He looked at me with questioning eyes and said, "Randi, what do you do, search for the dogs in the worst condition? This one is as bad as it gets. I don't even know if she can be helped. It looks like gangrene is setting in on her right side."

"I know, Jeff, but she seems so sweet. I'll take her to a vet on the way home. Please."

Jeff always succumbed to my requests and signed her card, releasing her to me while giving me unwanted and unnecessary authoritarian advice.

"I already know you're crazy, Randi," he said. "You know she could cost you a fortune, but it's your call. She'll need to be isolated. Good luck in finding a vet who can treat her. Your hands will be tied for awhile with her and my other dog that you're taking. Keep me posted, but don't call me here in the middle of the night for help."

Jeff's wry sense of humor amused me, and I knew that he would be more than thrilled to hear my voice at 4 a.m., whining to him about my rescues.

I grabbed the two kennel cards from Jeff's hands and playfully said, "I love you!" as I ran off to the front of the shelter to do the paper work and to pay for my two new rescue dogs.

By the time I left the shelter, I had already named this little girl April to celebrate the beginning of her new life in this month. But Jeff was right. The prognosis for April's healing was bleak, and every vet I went to said that there was nothing that could be done for her.

I continued my search for a vet who would disagree. My thoughts were consumed by the hopeful vision of seeing April gallop with carefree abandonment one day very soon.

Dr. Jim Craig in Encino had helped with many of my rescue dogs and found solutions for "problems" that were deemed hopeless or too costly to treat by other veterinarians. He had a rugged, outdoorsy, direct way about him and didn't like to waste time making things too complicated. When I placed April on his examining table, he took one look at her and then stared at me, through the top of his glasses, for what felt like ten minutes. Finally he spoke.

"Randi, what did you do to this dog?"

"Nothing! I just rescued her like this from a shelter!"

He cut me off, saying, "Why? Never mind. I'll see what we can do, but you'll have to be bringing her in every few days for awhile." Dr. Craig was my hero.

Dr. Craig saw more of me in the next month than he probably would have liked. But he was also now on a mission to do whatever it took to see April survive and live a normal, healthy life. He was unable to stay detached and was taking April's recovery to heart.

When I brought April back to him after her first skin graft and he removed the bandages, he seemed to be mad at himself. "Damn it, I don't know what went wrong. I don't know what else I could have done differently. You'll have to bring her back in a few days, and we'll try again." He abruptly left the room with his head down, swearing under his breath at himself.

Three days later, when I carried April back into Dr. Craig's office and he saw the long gash on her side, oozing with pus, he stared up at me from under his glasses and said, "Don't worry, Randi, we'll get through this. She is such a nice little dog. I'll figure something out."

Surgery after surgery, with constant follow-up care, saved April's life. The following weeks, I gave her many medications. No matter what this little girl had to endure, she never complained or raised a lip. April was an angel as a patient and a pleasure to have in my life. She was a complete lady at all times, contrasting with the scarred Frankenstein body she was now wearing.

Although April's treatment was finished and her life was no longer at risk, Dr. Craig wasn't sure if her scars would be forever visible. As sweet as April was, she would be difficult to place in a new home if that was the case.

I began bringing April to my open house dog adoptions dressed in charming sweaters, adorned with bows, but when the unveiling time came for those who were interested in her, the reaction of horror remained steady. The snappy little purebreds in perfect packages were quickly being adopted over my beautiful April. It almost felt demoralizing to continue subjecting her to such reactions, but I knew someone would see April with the same eyes as I did.

Weeks later, a soft-spoken, middle-aged-sounding woman named Ruth phoned and said, "I would like to adopt a sweet, gentle little female dog to be my lifetime companion. I'm at home much of the time, and I volunteer at a church. If she's mild-mannered, I could bring her with me."

Ruth's demeanor reminded me so much of April's that I had to take one more chance and tell Ruth the story. Ruth softly said, "Well, I don't mind if April remains scarred just as long as she isn't suffering." But Ruth hadn't seen April yet.

Upon our meeting, I was taken aback at how much alike April and Ruth seemed to be, both graced by an angelic femininity. I was even more stunned that April's unveiling this time received no reaction at all. Ruth, like me, saw beneath April's scars.

When the two drove off together, I'll never forget the heaviness in my heart as I watched April's face staring back at me until I was out of her sight. Although I was elated for April, I was hoping her departure wasn't as difficult for her as it was for me.

This proved to be true. Several days later, Ruth phoned and said, "I was getting a little worried about April because she seemed so sad and wouldn't eat. But now she won't leave my side and follows me everywhere, while staring at me. Thank you so much, Randi. She is such a dear, sweet girl."

Months later, Ruth again phoned and said, "Randi, April misses you and asked me if we could come and visit you at one of your adoptions. We would both love to see you again."

That following weekend, when Ruth proudly came walking up to me at my adoptions with an unfamiliar dog, I screamed out in rapture and ran up to her, hugging her, when I realized that April had been blessed with the most full, gorgeous, apricot coat of curls, covering her scars from another life.

That night, as I was filing away April's adoption papers, I began flipping through hundreds of dog photos and adoption contracts, each telling a story that held the key to my heart since I started my career of dog rescue five years earlier. Once again, my mind drifted back to life after Lucky and Skippy and the beginning of my dog rescuing days.

April Loved

CHAPTER 3

TRICK OR TREAT
October 31, 1987

Skippy had died only months earlier. I felt as though my soul had left with his. I no longer had a reason to stay in Encino, but I also had no specific destiny in mind if I left. I was now sure of only one thing in my life—that I needed to set myself free. Free from the pain of having watched Skippy slip away. Free from my brief life of miniscule accomplishments. And free from my apathy and indecisiveness for which society would be judging me, if I cared enough to listen.

I had always been able to rise higher than an eagle after falling—until now. I wasn't familiar with this side of myself, and the only action I felt comfortable taking was to run away from it. So, when my sister, Julie, now living in England, returned for the summer, I jumped at the opportunity to join her and a group of her hippie friends in a cross-country trip to a Rainbow Gathering in North Carolina. I didn't even know what a Rainbow Gathering was, but I knew it was something I needed to do—until I arrived.

I had spent the majority of my life in Encino, where credit cards, mirrors, posh lavatories, hair spray, blow dryers, and four-inch-high

Welcome to the Rainbow Gathering

Cherokee clogs were a way of life. I had recently graduated from California State University, Northridge as a proud, staunch, die-hard college Republican.

As the old, red pickup truck that safely transported a group of us from the San Fernando Valley to North Carolina slowly crept up the steep mountain to the Nantahala National Forest, we were met with an enormous, glittery rainbow-colored sign that greeted us with the words, "WELCOME HOME." This sign represented the beginning of anarchy, where police officers were prohibited as were plumbing, electricity, and money. Credit cards were unknown in this world. Clothing was optional as were any and all drugs. I was instantly struck with a severe case of homesickness when the first human I saw was a beer-bellied biker barbecuing in the buff. The marijuana cigarette falling out of the side of his mouth added to the unabashed joie de vivre he was experiencing. Encino, why did you let me leave you?

Julie danced off with her friends, and I found myself standing alone in a rainstorm as I watched a colony of naked bodies scurry away into their tents for cover. As a college Republican, I only stayed in the most elite hotels. I barely even knew what a tent was, and I certainly didn't happen to have one stashed away in my purse. Even if I did, I would not have known how to assemble it. Yes, I know they come with directions, but I could never be bothered with such things as reading through an instruction manual.

So, I was basically stranded on the top of a mountain in North Carolina with twenty thousand drug-infested, naked bodies. The hair spray that molded my hair into my perfect Farrah Fawcett do was melting down my shoulders. My black eyeliner, dripping down my face, now looked like Indian war paint on my cheeks. My four-inch-high Cherokee clogs were useless now that they were soggy and buried in mud. I was displaced, humbled, and hoping to bump into a police officer who had violated the Rainbow Gathering rules. A nice, clean-cut, fully clothed, Republican police officer would be my knight in shining armor who could rescue me from this ghastly fiasco.

But, as expected, luck was not on my side, and my police officer never arrived. The rainstorm blended with my tears, and I spent the next two hours sobbing out every emotion that my repressed and uptight ego had tried to bury for the last twenty-four years.

As the storm lifted, and the naked bodies began slowly to emerge from their tents, Julie—fully clothed, thank God!—found me. She wasn't quite sure what happened to me but, nonetheless, took pity and found someone to donate an assembled tent so that I could find refuge in my own private, much-needed space.

On the third day of my Rainbow Gathering adventure, Julie came to see if I was still alive. No one knew if anyone was in my tent because I only left it to urinate at 4 a.m. in one of the "posh," designated bathroom holes that had been dug out of the mud. My body-building training forced my mind into believing that, until I had a nice private bathroom with plumbing, no other bodily functions existed.

When I heard Julie's voice outside my tent singing, "Randi, are you in there? Wake up! I have a surprise for you," I felt a sense of relief, as if I were back home in Encino. I hadn't spoken in two days and thought I might have forgotten how to but easily answered her as though I was as good as gold. "Droolie? (That was my nickname for her because she drooled in her sleep as a child.) Droolie?"

"What are you doing?" she asked.

"I've been in here writing for the past couple of days. Come in."

She cracked open the tent, and a little tan, scruffy terrier came bounding up to me, drenching my face in kisses.

"This is a magic, healing dog, who wanted to come and meet you," she said. "I thought he would make you feel better."

I didn't think there were any tears left inside of me but, once again, I was wrong. I wrapped my arms around his wriggling body and never wanted to let him go. He did indeed feel magical, but then again, any dog at this time in my life would have.

She left him with me for about an hour and when she returned, she said, "Okay. I have to take him back to his dad now."

She pulled him out of my arms and danced off into the woods, with the echo of the bells entwined in her long red dreadlocks trailing behind her.

I was confused, calling out to her when she had already danced too far away to hear me, "Are you having some sort of a drug overdose? Why would you bring me a dog, pretend like he was meant to be mine, and then yank him away from me? If it isn't the negative effect of some hallucinogen, then you definitely have a severe cognitive problem that is impairing your judgment."

Julie was obviously lacking the insight to notice my fragile, emotional state. Or maybe she just didn't care. Whichever it was, I would now have to venture out of my tent to go find my magic, healing dog.

Before I left Encino, I had stuffed my oversized purse with protein bars. I would have been more than content rationing them and hiding out in my tent for the next two weeks. As I threw on a pair of jeans, a ripped sweatshirt, and tennis shoes, I pondered exiting my tent in the light of the day and facing some of these "people."

Is *everyone* here naked? I wondered. Would they be imposing their nakedness on me with their hippie hugs? Would I be expected to take drugs with them? And, most important, if people were going to walk around naked in public, why wouldn't they work out? Have they no shame?

While my mind continued, I slowly cracked open my tent and was blinded by the sunlight that I hadn't seen in days. I peeked my head out and was even more blinded by a man walking by, wearing only moccasins and a fig leaf. After he was far enough away for me to feel safe, I did it! I was standing outside my tent on the knoll overlooking a menagerie of scattered "Halloween" parties that all comprised the makings of a Rainbow Gathering. I could see a large circle of people playing bongo drums, a village of Indian teepees, a village of school buses, an alcoholics camp, a women's-only camp, a men's only camp, a fairy camp for kids, a Jewish camp where Friday night services were held, and a barter row. The scenes were endless, all labeled by huge signs to guide people to their desired destinations. It appeared that everyone was blissfully coexisting in this world without rules, judgments, and egos. Three days ago I absolutely would not have fit in anywhere. But, now purged of everything I had known myself to be, I was able to begin drifting inconspicuously down the knoll where I had been standing for the last forty-five minutes.

As I was making my descent down the dirt trails through the woods and into the masses, "Jesus" appeared before me: a tall, slim man with long, wavy dark hair and crystal blue eyes. He was wearing only gauze, genie-like belly-dancing pants and sandals made out of thick rope. He floated up to me, violating my personal space as though we knew each other well, and stared directly into my eyes, whispering to me, "Peace, sister."

What was I supposed to do? I really had nothing to say to Jesus. As a college Republican, I was used to shaking hands when meeting someone, and we all respected each other enough to keep that safe, three feet of distance between us. But I'm sure Jesus knew nothing about any of this. He probably didn't even vote!

I politely smiled and reached out my hand to shake his.

"Hi," I said. "You look like Jesus."

He responded with a calm, inner tranquility. "I've heard that before. Are you enjoying yourself?"

"I'm not sure. I just spent my first days here alone. I really needed to be alone. I'm very discerning about the people I invite into my space."

I had hoped that he would get the hint and back up a foot or two, but instead, he leaned in closer to me, gently taking my hands into his and said, with his soothing tone of voice, "I understand, and well you should be. What is your name?"

I think Jesus hypnotized me with his piercing blue eyes because I don't remember any of the rest of our conversation until he floated away, whispering, "Randi, you are very rich."

Three days ago, I would have responded with, "I don't feel very rich. I can't even use my credit cards here. Where is the nearest five-star hotel?" But now I found myself wishing for Jesus to float back to me. I wasn't done with him.

Jesus did indeed hypnotize me into feeling as if I was floating, just like him. And, as far as I knew, he did not force any drugs on me. Something happened, but I wasn't sure what. I couldn't wait to get into the "menagerie" and find more people just like Jesus.

I was smiling at everyone, clothed or not. People were inviting me into their drumming circles, tepees, and buses. Two days later on the Fourth of July, I stood in a circle with thousands of people, all joining hands and praying for world peace.

I went to barter row and traded a protein bar for a tie-dyed gauze skirt. I volunteered to watch people's dogs in exchange for tarot card readings and rainbow hair wraps embellished with feathers, beads, and bells, just like Julie. I had completely forgotten about my magic, healing dog. I had so many offers from all sorts of different people wanting me to travel through the country with them after the Rainbow Gathering that I wasn't the least bit concerned if I never found Julie and her friends again. Anything would have been better than traveling back to California with seven people crammed into a small pickup truck.

Everyone was asking me which drug I had taken. When I always responded by saying, "My mind," most of them either looked at me confused or laughed as their eyes rolled back into their heads, while walking away. Indeed, I felt as if I had been given a lobotomy and for the first time was experiencing life without my overly judgmental mind. For me, this was greater than any drug I could have ingested.

As the painted school buses, multicolored campsites, and colonies of now fully clothed hippies, weighted down by extra-large back packs, began to fade into the sunset, and the Nantahala National Forest was respectfully being put back into its original condition, I found myself deliriously lying in the last remaining campsite of the 1987 Rainbow Gathering, a makeshift hospital. I had contracted a severe case of dysentery from drinking the water in the forest. I now had a fever of 102 degrees, hadn't seen Julie in days, and was unable to walk.

When I awoke, I found myself in a boat that was being towed by a truck. I looked up to a man standing over me wearing a cowboy hat, blue jeans, a brassiere and a cape that had the words Kaptain Kao written on it. He was holding a spoon with pink liquid on it and said, "Here, Randi, it's time for your medicine."

Apparently I was at a harbor in New Jersey and now on tour with the Grateful Dead.

Roy was a middle-aged family man who lived in Mill Valley, California. While on a business trip in San Diego, he stopped to pick up some stranded hitchhikers, and they talked him into abandoning his mundane life for an exciting summer touring with the Grateful Dead. How I became part of this, I do not know. But many Rainbow Gathering attendees continued the festivities by touring with the Grateful Dead. I guess, in the midst of my dysentery delirium, I became one of them.

Roy took on the father role and nurtured those of us with ailing intestinal tracts. We lovingly named him Kaptain Kaopectate and made him a cape as an expression of our appreciation. We toured with the Grateful Dead in luxury, riding in his boat that was being towed by his truck all throughout the country. Roy had the time of his life revisiting his crazy youth with us and would follow through with any dare we dangled before him. Hence, he was wearing a bra, jeans, and a cowboy hat in a New Jersey harbor.

At the end of the summer, I was reunited with Julie at a Grateful Dead show in Berkeley, California, which was close to Roy's hometown. I had been transformed into a hippie—at least for a while—and spent the last show with Julie reminiscing about our summer.

I hadn't a clue as to what I was going to do with the rest of my life. Julie would be going back to Europe, and for me, the thought of returning to Encino, where my dark memories would again thrive, had no appeal whatsoever.

I had spent a summer of celebration, burying everything I knew. I had even buried my thoughts about Skippy. I wanted nothing in my life that could remind me of him.

I thought I had no attachments until I heard the prophetic yelping of a dog in pain after being hit by a car. Everything I had just spent the summer running away from was instantly reborn, and I knew I had to face my greatest fear and return home.

While back in Encino, I spent my first few days making a futile attempt at surviving without canine energy while I began to pursue a career in acting. Soon after, I realized that the only thing that had ever given me complete fulfillment for seventeen of my twenty-four years was the sacred spirit of a dog.

Although I was not there for Skippy and Lucky through many of those years, they had continued to love me unconditionally. I needed this and began my search to find the one thing I knew my life could not do without.

I returned to Lucky and Skippy's shelter, hoping to see one of them sitting there again as the puppy I knew when I was a child.

What I ended up connecting with was nothing like Lucky or Skippy.

"Can you tell me anything about that one that's hiding behind the others?" I asked a kennel worker.

"Well, she has several red checks on her card," the worker said. "It looks like this was a mistake. She was supposed to have been put to sleep twice. Let me check on her." She walked away, looking confused.

She returned ten minutes later with the rest of the dog's story. "She was turned in by her owners because they moved. She could have been put to sleep after only an hour, but we've kept her for over two months now. It seems she's got a fan club here who keeps taking her off of the euthanasia list. We would love for you to take her. We know she's kind of funny looking, but she's got a great personality."

When I saw her name, Inky, on the kennel card and called it out, she cocked her goat-like head at me, emerged from behind several larger, intimidating dogs, and began dancing with joy. Inky was a medium-size, half-terrier, half-goat-looking breed, black with frizzy, unkempt fur, and a physique that resembled a sausage wearing toothpicks for legs. She had a long goatee streaked with gray, and she looked like an old Jewish rabbi.

The kennel workers were clapping, and it seemed that all the dogs were howling with joy and cheering Inky on when she strutted down the kennel with me, finally safe and freed from prison, as my new life mate.

Although I would hear comments from people whispering to each other as they passed us on the street—"That's the ugliest dog I've ever seen"—Inky was, and always would be, my beauty queen. She felt like my right arm, and I knew our souls began together. The sacred spirits of Lucky and Skippy lived on in Inky.

Within a week, I found myself back at that same animal shelter. There were a few other faces there that I couldn't get out of my mind, and when I realized that I was no longer that seven-year-old girl with my dad saying, "No, Randi, you can only pick one," I had to return.

I didn't quite understand what it meant when the kennel workers kept saying, "This one is on the list." So, now that I was more able to focus, I needed to find out.

As I walked through the hallways lined with cages packed full of dogs on either side of me, my seven-year-old mind returned, and I again thought, "I want them all, but now no one can stop me."

My mom and dad were now divorced, and my mom was the sucker who used to sleep outside with Nanny, our goat.

"Hmm," I said to myself. "I bet I can bring a few more dogs home and she wouldn't even notice."

Inky-My beauty queen

I pulled aside the kennel worker who had helped me with Inky and pointed to a little dog who must have been part monkey because it was hanging upside down from the top of its cage.

"I love this one too. Can you tell me more about him?"

She pulled the kennel card and said, "Oh no. It's not a him. It's a female schnauzer who looks like she's in heat. No wonder she's climbing the cage. Someone made a mistake and put her in this cage full of unneutered males."

I jumped in, cutting her off, and said, "Then I need to take her too. She needs help. By the way, what does 'on the list' mean?"

"Well, it means that a dog's time is up and it's going to be put to sleep."

"But how come you said every dog's time is up that I ask you about? Why do they have to put any of them to sleep anyway?" I naively asked.

"We don't have room to keep them all. New ones come in every day, so many more than the number that gets adopted. We always have to put about seventy-five percent of them to sleep," she replied, without making any eye contact with me.

I couldn't believe it, and it didn't make sense to me. I also couldn't ignore it. I called my mom on the way out of the shelter, carrying Inky's new sister under my arm.

My mom said, "Absolutely not! We just got Inky less than a week ago. Do not bring another dog home." I was shocked that my sucker mom stood up to me. She never said no.

I spent the rest of the day in search of a "no-kill" shelter that would take my new dog. Pet Adoption Fund offered to take her in for me and, when I left her there that afternoon, I spent another hour looking at all of the other dogs that I wanted to bring home. I didn't ever want to leave.

One of their volunteers, Marsha, came up to me and asked, "Do you wanna come with me and help rescue a dog that was thrown off a truck? He's been abandoned and has no owner."

I excitedly accepted and followed Marsha to the house in my own car. As we approached the neighborhood where this dog had been loitering for the past few days, my eyes met with what looked more like a four-month-old bucking bronco than a dog. We got out of our cars and spent the next hour playing hide-and-seek with this "dog," trying to catch him. Marsha was gasping for air and we were both ready to collapse when we finally lassoed him with a leash. He wouldn't stop bucking, so she fell to the ground, throwing her entire body over him.

She looked up at me while gasping for air and said, "Someone in the neighborhood saw a truck pull up, the door open, and this puppy come flying out. All the neighbors said he's now terrified of cars. Why don'tcha foster him? He's just gonna be in a cage otherwise."

"Are you kidding?" I said in disbelief. "This bucking bronco will give himself a concussion if he's stuck in a cage."

I don't remember saying yes, but Marsha had that strong New York, sweet, manipulative way about her and began shoving him into my car.

"Hey, Ran…give me a hand here. He's cute, isn't he? Looks like a Snickers candy bar. That's what you should name him."

I got in my car, and she slammed the door shut, almost on my leg. Marsha couldn't wait to get out of there and waved at me as I drove away with my first foster dog, a shaggy bearded collie mix, soon to be named Snickers.

Driving down Ventura Boulevard with Snickers in the car felt like being on the inside of a pinball machine. He was completely hysterical and flailing himself against all of the windows. When I pulled into my garage and got out of my car, I was bruised and drenched in perspiration. How would I explain this to my mom?

When I opened the door to let him in the house, it was like the first tornado that had ever hit Encino, California. Inky, with her calm, wise demeanor, curiously but cautiously trotted up to him with her tail wagging.

"What is that?" she asked me with her eyes.

When my mom heard all of the commotion and came into the kitchen to see who was ransacking her house, she smiled and said, "Oh my God!" while reaching her arms out for him. He leaped up into the air, hitting her in the jaw, but she didn't care. All she wanted to do was hug him.

"So, does that mean you're not kicking me out?" I asked. "He had nowhere else to go."

"We'll have to keep him then," she said.

I couldn't believe it.

Snickers looking for trouble

Within a few days, my mom had fallen in love with Snickers, but my canine soul mate, Inky, and I agreed that this hyperactive, insensitive, selfish foster dog had overstayed his visit. He wasn't one of those dogs who just liked to kiss—he would molest you with his mouth.

Our patience had run out with him. Every shoe I owned had Snickers' teeth marks in it, and Inky was not amused when Snickers would dive-bomb off the bed onto her. It felt as if fate had played a cruel trick on Inky and me. I returned him to Pet Adoption Fund where Marsha volunteered, and thanked God I was free of him. It seemed I was the only one who didn't think that Snickers was cute. They didn't live with him.

It took my mom several days to begin speaking to me again and to forgive me for getting rid of the love of her life.

As the weeks passed, I had gotten in the habit of visiting Pet Adoption Fund, helping out or bringing other dogs I had rescued from death row. I began to wonder why Snickers hadn't been adopted as he was pretty cute (if you didn't get to know him too well). I tried pushing him on prospective adopters as I sadly saw the puppy in him fading away. Adult dogs are never as adoptable as the cute, bouncy puppies.

It was All Hallow Eve, October 31, 1987, and pouring rain. Snickers had been lost in the shuffle of two hundred other dogs and after months, still not adopted.

"Do you know where Snickers is?" I asked one of the women working at Pet Adoption Fund.

"Who?" she responded.

"Snickers, the cute young bearded collie mix. I fostered him," I impatiently said.

"I'm sorry. I don't know which dog you're talking about. You're free to go look for him, though," she replied, going through her stack of paperwork.

The kennel was closing, and a family had come in to exchange a dog they had adopted for a livelier, more playful one. Boy, did I have a match for them! In the downpour of rain, I rushed to go looking for Snickers and found him buried in a room with about six bigger dogs. What happened to the obnoxious Snickers that I so disliked? As I dug him out of the pile of dogs and carried him through the rain to meet his prospective new family, I looked into his eyes and saw a broken spirit.

This family did think he was cute, but adopted another more desperate dog with more energy. As the family signed the adoption agreement and left with their new companion, Snickers had fallen asleep in my lap. I couldn't bring myself to wake him only to put him back in the over-crowded room where his spirit had died. I had no choice but to beg the people at Pet Adoption Fund to let me take him home.

As I again pulled into my garage with Snickers, my new perfect angel, he threw up all over my car. I carried him inside, and my mom grabbed him from me, took him to her bedroom, and put him on her bed, hugging him all the while. "Look what you did to him," she said. "You are never to take him away from here again."

We spent the next two months nursing him back to health, and by this time, we had all accepted him for better or for worse. Snickers became one with us and our home.

My addiction to animal shelters grew, and as the number of dogs in our house fluctuated on a daily basis, I saw Inky now looking to Snickers for protection. This worked wonders for his ego, although it did seem as if he could never get enough human love.

When I finally found homes for all of our canine sleepovers from animal shelters, I thought it was time to take the "kids" camping and broaden their horizons. I still yearned to return to my carefree life as a hippie and decided to go to a Grateful Dead show in Monterey, California.

When Roy was towing his boat through New Jersey, wearing his cowboy hat and brassiere, we were hopelessly lost one afternoon. We stopped a girl on the street to ask for directions and she was so amused that she ended up joining us for a part of the summer. Deanna and I became the greatest of friends, and she flew out from New Jersey to rekindle our sisterhood and the grandest summer of our lives.

Before leaving for Monterey, Deanna and I prepared Snickers with little car journeys in advance, hoping to relieve some of his hysteria, but it always ended with my car being decorated from his vomit. We left in the middle of the night, hoping "the kids" would sleep through our seven-hour drive. Inky was out in about five minutes. Snickers thought he had died and gone to Hell but finally fell asleep after four hours on the road. I was in awe as we arrived to an incredibly majestic campground in the heart of Monterey. We were surrounded by towering pines, crisp, clean air, and the irreplaceable music of the Grateful Dead. This was as good as life got, or so I thought.

I realized Inky would be taking care of herself, and unfortunately, Snickers had many more obnoxious behaviors I hadn't yet experienced. There were many other dogs here with their peaceful hippie parents, but Snickers decided he and Inky should be the only ones enjoying this ride and would do everything in his power to make this happen. He particularly enjoyed fighting with the large, muscular, unneutered male dogs wearing spiked collars and roaming alone. Snickers was about the sweetest, most innocent-looking dog at our campground, but within a couple days, we heard people whispering to each other as they would turn around to avoid us, "There's that mean little dog." He seemed to have quite a high opinion of himself with the female dogs (and some males) and couldn't comprehend why they all didn't graciously accept him on top of them. I seriously considered tying him to a tree and driving away (we all get what we deserve in life), but he had mastered chewing or breaking through anything in seconds, all just to be with me—what an honor. If I took more than five steps away from him, the show he put on paralleled that of a dog being severely beaten to a pulp. These were the first signs of what was soon to become hard-core separation anxiety.

We had corrupted the energy of this peaceful scene long enough and snuck away in the wee hours of the night when no one would see us. Snickers had grown attached to the tent life in the mountains, and I could see the pain on his face as we left. His hypersensitivity intensified with each new experience, causing him daily hardships. Inky flowed with life as though she created it herself.

Within a week of being home, Snickers became progressively worse. One early morning when I had just left home, I was driving along Ventura Boulevard and saw something out of the corner of my eye. I looked closer and realized that it was Snickers, running along the sidewalk trying to follow me in my car. He now began breaking out of windows and doors and running away several times a day to find trouble in the neighborhood.

Snickers' separation anxiety destroyed every material object I forgot to hide. My sanity was fading. I spoke to trainers who, after meeting Snickers, said, "We really suggest you have him euthanized. These behavior problems are beyond the realm of anything that can be corrected." I ignored them, assuming that they were all ignorant, incompetent, and inexperienced.

I had recently begun volunteering at and then working for Pet Orphans Fund, a nonprofit animal rescue organization in Van Nuys. They had a very experienced and patient trainer, Sandi Wirth, who was holding classes at the facility. She also trained animals for the movies. When I spoke with Sandi on the phone, she was very encouraging and I was comfortable with her gentleness. Snickers ducked down anytime someone approached him, indicating that he had been hit. As obnoxious as he was, I didn't want anyone being too harsh with him or harming him in any way.

Sandi invited Snickers and me to her classes but when we arrived, she stared at us in shock. Snickers was foaming at the mouth while barking, growling, and attacking anything and everything he could see. It was utter chaos. After the second week, I dropped out, feeling embarrassed and frustrated. Both Snickers and I had failed training.

The year was now 1989, and Snickers was still in my life, unaffected by neutering and an attempt at training. I was sick with bronchitis, and the socialization of Snickers was at the bottom of my list of priorities. I needed to let go of my hostility toward him. Oddly, during this time he began to tune into my needs and never left my side while I was sick. I began to accept him for what he was, not what I thought he should be. With our newfound understanding, I asked Sandi if we could try one of her classes again.

"Please do," she said. "I will help you in any way I can, Randi. We can work through this."

Sandi had an entire crew of groupies who were so very fond of her. People would bring her gifts years after their dogs had graduated. Her classes always felt like a party that no one ever wanted to see end.

When I brought Snickers back to class, my desperation to change him having faded, it turned out that his desperation to control things, causing his aggression, had also lessened. Snickers was excited to be working with me now, and we began to flow so well together that everyone could see him developing. Snickers needed enthusiasm and unconditional love. I had been giving him the opposite. Now we were in class

Snickers at three

for the shared experience of learning together, and I became the one with separation anxiety whenever I had to be away from him.

Snickers won second place at graduation and became a sensitive and compassionate caretaker for the many abused and neglected dogs I continued to rescue. Sandi asked us to return and join her in helping to teach her classes.

After that, Snickers finished advanced training with movie behaviors, completed two commercials, acted in his first film, and won an array of trophies. No words could do justice to describe the high I felt working with Snickers. I'm sure he was hoping that someone would finally understand him and give him what he needed so that he could become a happy, self-actualized dog.

Snickers launched my rescuing career, and because of him, I've always held a special place in my heart for rescuing and rehabilitating the many abused and neglected dogs who are labeled unsalvageable. Once understood, these are the dogs that become the world's most loyal life mates.

I see many people give up dogs that are crying out for help. Many destructive and aggressive dogs may be a reflection of how we are dealing with them and, if turned into some animal shelters by their owners, may be destroyed after only one hour.

When I catch myself losing my patience, I often reflect on my journey with Snickers. When I refused to give up on him, he slowly began to change—or did I?

Snickers finely aged at 16!

CHAPTER 4

THANKSGIVING 1989

Thanksgiving of 1989 snuck into my life so quickly that I hadn't even realized my budding career as a dog rescuer was now in full bloom.

Where humans once sat encircling the Thanksgiving spread now sat our honored canine guests who would have otherwise been homeless or in heaven. Inky and Snickers were now accompanied by our four-legged foster family, who would be celebrating this Thanksgiving with us at our four-star mutt motel.

It seemed that everyone who had adopted a dog from me hoped to turn this into a reunion and join us for this enchanted evening. But Thanksgiving was now a very formal occasion, at least for the dogs, and only those who could leave their judgments at the door were invited. Our plush, comfortable chairs were now reserved for the canine guests, and any humans who joined us for this and all future Thanksgiving traditions would have to be amenable to serving the four-legged "royalty." Needless to say, very few humans were welcomed, as most were insulted at the idea of sitting on the floor or catering to a clan of overly spoiled "recycled pets."

My mom had always dreaded entertaining at her house, and after the times that she did, she would usually end up sprawled out on her bed, breathing into a paper bag from the stress. But now, entertaining had taken on an entirely new meaning for her. This Thanksgiving, she was up at the crack of dawn, and I was the one who almost passed out when I came into the kitchen to find her cheerfully cooking and singing to our overextended four-legged family. The kitchen was filled with rear ends wagging against each other and heads cocking in all directions with their undivided attention on my mom, who, it seemed, had been possessed by the spirit of Mary Poppins. For a variety of reasons, three in particular, this Thanksgiving would be the most unforgettable one of my life.

Hundreds of homeless dogs now crossed my path every week at the animal shelters I couldn't resist visiting. Of course, I had no interest in rescuing most of the easy, normal cases. The young, bouncing, happy dogs everyone else was ogling did nothing for me. I had to search for the most pitiful and depressed dogs I could find. These dogs would be a challenge for me. These were the dogs with the red checks on their cards, meaning that they were on the list to be "put to sleep." And some of these dogs would be the ones whose faces would appear in our Thanksgiving photos for the rest of their lives.

I had all but forgotten about my dream of finding Lucky or Skippy at the animal shelter from which they both came as puppies. But one day, when I was visiting that same shelter, I was stopped dead in my tracks while rushing past all of the cages, and I ended up in the hospital section that held the injured dogs.

Could my Rainbow Gathering days have fooled me? It seemed I was hallucinating or having a flashback from the drugs I thought I never ingested, when I saw Skippy sitting in the exact same cage he had been in five years earlier after being hit by a car. I had to do a double take. I had heard that lack of sleep could cause hallucinations such as these, but I stood in front of this cage long enough to realize that something quite bizarre and very real had just occurred.

I pulled the kennel card off the cage and read, "*Tan, border terrier mix. Hit by car, White Oak Avenue.*" When Skippy was hit by the car five years earlier, it was also on White Oak Avenue. This was more than I needed to know that this dog was coming home with me.

I went searching for one of the veterinary technicians who had been treating him and handed the kennel card to the first one I found—a very serious man, wearing a white veterinary jacket. I smiled and asked, "Can you sign this dog off to me? I'd like to take him."

"I'm sorry," he said. "You cannot take this dog home. He has a concussion, and we cannot release him until his waiting period is up. He came in as a stray, and his owner may be looking for him. If his owner doesn't claim him, we will then have to put him to sleep. He's been vomiting and is not responding to any medication or attention."

"But I want to take him," I begged this man, whom I was quickly beginning to dislike. "I will take him no matter how sick he is. I don't care what is wrong with him."

"I'm sorry, ma'am. I cannot release him to you. If he continues to vomit, we will have to put him to sleep before his waiting period is up."

For the sake of Skippy's reincarnation, I did not verbalize my thoughts: "I would be vomiting too if I had to be around you for long." Instead, I forced myself to remain cordial and asked, "Is there anything I can do so you won't put him to sleep?"

"Well, ma'am, you can call and check on him daily. If we know someone is seriously interested in him, we may hold off euthanizing him, but there are no guarantees. He will be available in three days if he doesn't get any sicker."

I went back to see my new Skippy, who just sat leaning against the back of his cage. His body was covered in mild abrasions, and he would not make any eye contact with me. Either he really was sick, or the veterinary technician's depressing personality had worn off on him. Whichever it was, I would not let this dog be euthanized.

All I could think of for the next three days was cupping my hands over the top of this dog's little bumpy head and doing whatever it took to make him feel better. I was unable to sleep for those three days, thinking of him sitting in that cage, depressed and possibly in pain.

On the day he was to be available, I arrived at the shelter fifteen minutes early, at 7:45 a.m., hoping that he would still be there. With my heart racing, I marched into the hospital section and up to Skippy's cage to see my new dog. He was sitting up, leaning against the back of it. Although he was still unresponsive and would not make eye contact with anyone, he had stopped vomiting.

As I carried him out of the shelter, the seven-year-old girl in me returned. It felt as if both Lucky and Skippy were coming home again.

I immediately took him to Dr. Deborah Hoffman's veterinary clinic, and when I carried him up to the counter, both Dr. Hoffman and her assistant Mary said, "Wow! We know why you took this one. That's unbelievable."

Upon examining and x-raying him, Dr. Hoffman said, "It looks like he is fine and does not have any internal injuries. But it does seem that he is very hand-shy and fearful. His abrasions are minor and will heal within the week. I just can't figure out why he won't walk."

After bringing him home, it became quite apparent to me that this dog had been very abused and had no desire to reach out to anyone. I had never seen a dog who seemed so alone and who did not want to be helped. My mom invited him up onto her bed, where he spent most of the next three months with his back against her, never facing her or making any eye contact.

This was the first new dog that Snickers immediately accepted and did not try to kill upon first sight. Both Inky and Snickers seemed to know to keep their distance from our new "Skippy" so as not to overwhelm him. They attempted gently to teach him how to play, but still, after a month, "Skippy" would not walk on his own, and I continued carrying him wherever I thought he needed to go.

Finally, one day when I had carried him into the kitchen, he slowly began crawling on the floor like a soldier, scooting along rough terrain, hiding out from his enemies. We all began watching him. For the first time, his tail started to wag. He spent over an hour scooting along the floor with his tail wagging and, over a week later, hadn't stopped except to eat and sleep. This was when we gave him his name—Skooter-Boo—and, after two months, we rejoiced in the very simple pleasure of watching him walk on his own.

Skooter-Boo's true confidence came when I put him in one of Sandi Wirth's obedience classes that Snickers and I were helping to teach. At first, Skooter reverted back to his depressed, fearful ways and, due to his insecurities and intimidation by the other dogs, would not walk during the "heeling" part of the ten-week course. But by graduation, he

Skooter bonding with Snickers

Skooter-Boo
with first place trophy

had triumphed and became the proudest, most self-assured dog in the class, receiving a first-place trophy! This was when his full name became Skooter-Boo 200 IQ, and he began staring at people with the intensity of a philosopher.

Although Skooter was only about a year old when I rescued him, he never did act like a young dog. We discovered that he was a mild hypochondriac and would become stressed from too much noise or too many dogs crowding around him. This would cause him to suffer from an upset stomach, which is why he was vomiting in the shelter. He was a very serious, deep, and complex being who seemed to sit back and analyze each situation with his big inquisitive eyes before jumping in and making decisions. Many people commented that it seemed he was looking straight through them and into their souls.

But if Skooter-Boo had been difficult, Buster, a bearded collie mix with basset hound legs, was my true challenge. Volunteers from an animal shelter had called me to rescue other dogs who had red checks on their kennel cards and were on the list to be euthanized. I went to the shelter several times within that week and had noticed one particular dog who seemed never to move from his spot in the cage. I was rushing to rescue all of the other dogs the volunteers had phoned me about when I finally stopped long enough to see if this dog was even alive. I noticed that the other dogs in his cage were urinating and walking on him. I went looking for someone to give me more information on this dog.

I tried to escape when Skooter's depressing veterinary technician walked toward me smiling. The "executioner" seemed to relish in giving me the grim news on this dog. "The gardener who worked at the house where this dog lived brought him to our shelter. He thought that the dog had been kept in a closet or a shed for years, never having been let out, living in his urine and feces. As you can see, he is so severely neglected that his matted fur is preventing him from walking. No one knows how old he is, but I would discourage you from rescuing him due to the extensive care he will need. Anyway, this one has been on our euthanasia list for days now. You really should just let him go."

As I was born with an incredibly strong will that revels in accomplishing tasks that other people label difficult, I now had to see if I could get this dog to respond to me. I had to prove "the executioner" wrong.

This tech was so apathetic about this dog that he would not even take him out of the cage for me to handle, so I spent nearly an hour just sitting by the cage, hoping that this dog would move. All of the other very adoptable dogs crowded around for my love, pawing at me and barking, but I knew these dogs were safe and not yet on the list to be put to sleep. I gave all of them a bit of fuss, but my focus was on the one that wouldn't awaken. I sat against that cage until the shelter closed and went home, feeling as though I had been defeated.

I spent that night awake, wondering if that was his last day alive. I was obsessed with him and had to return the next day to see if my worries were valid. My heart sang at the sight of his body, even though it again seemed as if he hadn't awakened since I had last seen him.

As I again sat by his cage, I prayed for him to give me some sign that he wanted to be rescued. After forty-five minutes, he slowly lifted his head and then his body. When I began to talk to him he crept over to me with his head down and leaned against the cage where I sat. I thanked him for coming to me. I had no idea what our future held, but I felt we already had won!

I left the shelter carrying the most physically and emotionally neglected dog I had ever seen. With tears streaming down my face, I promised him that he would never again be in this condition.

The first day with my new rescue dog proved to me that he was terrified of all light, noises, movement, and touch. Grooming him was like shearing a lamb because his mats were the size of footballs. It was also quite traumatic for him, and it seemed that all he wanted to do was run away and hide. Within the week, I gave him the name Buster as he resembled a dear friend's dog I met in Sandi's obedience classes with that name.

For nearly six months, Buster's fear kept him in a semicomatose state. He never moved or woke on his own. He had such intense nightmares that he could not catch his breath. I often wondered if he would slip away in his sleep in search of a less painful world.

As much as Buster did not want to move, I knew that I had to force him to take little steps or he would remain a vegetable and never gain self-confidence. I spent many afternoons holding him in my lap outside, simply exposing him to the sun, wind, and normal noises—all of which terrified him so much that he would fall asleep to avoid them.

Soon after that, I awoke one morning with Buster staring at me. This was the first time that Buster awoke on his own. A few weeks later, he jumped off the bed to drink water. This was the first time he had ever fulfilled a need for himself.

Skooter must have identified with him because he never left his side and helped him through each new risk. Skooter would wait to eat with him, and when Buster was too frightened to eat, Skooter brought him mouthfuls of kibble, running back and forth from the kitchen to my mom's bedroom where Buster lived, until his new friend was full. And, unbelievably, when Buster began walking on his own, Skooter-Boo 200 IQ would hold the doggie door open to help him out.

Over a year after Buster came to me, I knew that it was time to attempt Sandi's obedience classes. Buster would have preferred never to leave the house, but Sandi once again encouraged me by saying, "Randi, just bring him and let him watch for awhile. You need to expand his horizons in a slow, gentle way. He'll eventually come around. I promise."

As expected, Buster tried to hide most of the time we were in Sandi's classes. I sat off at a distance, simply holding him and watching. By the third week, Sandi urged me to begin integrating Buster, and as evil as I felt doing so, the experience slowly began to build his confidence as it had Skooter's. Within a month, Buster was so delighted to return home after each obedience class that he romped through the house, roaring like a lion, and finally began interacting with the rest of the family. Three weeks later, at Buster's graduation, no one would have ever guessed about the life he had survived before coming to me.

And then came a dumpy, pint-sized, petit basset griffon vendeen mix that I rescued from a shelter in the San Gabriel Valley. I found this chap pouting in the corner of his cage, very withdrawn, shy, and scheduled to be destroyed. He had been abused by a man and could not be touched from his waist to his tail without trying to bite. But when I took him out of his cage, he instantly lit up and began strutting in circles, punching me with his paws. I spent most of our car ride home with him in my lap. All the way, he sat up and begged, punched me in the face with his plump paws, or put his paws on the steering wheel, attempting to drive.

Before we reached Encino, I had fallen in love with this precocious little elf and stopped at my mom's office to show him off to everyone.

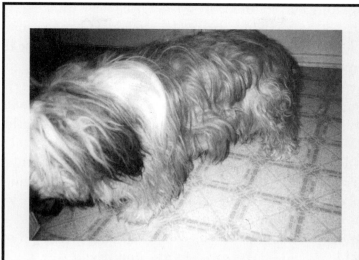

Buster-no will to live

The champion in
Buster lives

As I was lifting him out of my jeep, he wiggled loose from my arms and swaggered off to attack the parking lot attendant. I caught him before his jaw locked onto the man's leg. I already knew by this time that this sprightly handful had a mind of his own and would be giving me a run for my money.

I brought him in to meet my mom and all of her co-workers. He seemed to think he was some sort of celebrity, putting on a show and flirting with all of the women. He was sitting up, begging and waving before his crowd of fans, while looking around to make sure they all were giving him their undivided attention. Everyone was laughing until the door opened and a man peeked his head in to see what he was missing. The elf stopped performing and ran off to attack him.

My mom's law practice was completely insignificant to me compared with rescuing dogs, so I couldn't understand why she became angry and said, "Randi! I don't need to be sued in my own office for a dog bite. You know dogs aren't even supposed to be in here. Do not bring that biting dog to my house."

I left with my elf, both of us feeling a bit dejected. But we picked our spirits right back up, and I drove home with him in my lap, steering and waving out the window to any women who smiled at him. Then a man pulled up next to us at a red light and the elf almost broke out of my jeep, baring his teeth to attack him.

When my mom got home that night, she apologized to the elf and invited him into her room, where he spent the night asleep on her head.

Although my elf was extremely adoptable in my eyes, and everyone agreed that he was incredibly cute, most people were not as enthralled as I was by his precociousness. This is when I decided that I should name him, realizing that I would probably be his forever mother. I had a difficult time selecting a name that would do him justice. But, after several weeks, and taking a poll from over twenty people, the elf was given the name Rooney. He would accompany me almost everywhere so that I could work on socializing him with men. At least this was the reason I gave to people for favoring him over all of the other dogs. The truth was that I was thoroughly entertained by his imp-like antics and couldn't bear to be away from him.

It took months for Rooney to learn to trust men and not to attack them. We attempted obedience class, but he was more interested in

License and registration please, Rooney!

Rooney playing to his audience
on Halloween

being the class clown than competing for any trophies. One of our biggest "highs" was taking agility classes together, which seemed like a playground for dogs. But again Rooney was more interested in playing with the other dogs and causing trouble than winning anything. He became the honorary "class troublemaker" when he disappeared and the instructor and I found him climbing down the windshield of a car parked by the agility course.

Before Rooney realized that not all men were evil, he was responsible for my first driving ticket. We were on the freeway, and he was sitting up begging and waving at me from the passenger seat, doing everything he could to get my attention. After all, I was ignoring him while I was paying attention to the road. In Rooney's world, this was sinful. His eleventh commandment was "Thou shalt never ignore me." When I realized that I was sinning and began to fawn over him, tickling his distended tummy and shaking his pudgy paw, I almost missed our off-ramp. I looked in the rearview mirror and saw that there were no cars in sight. So I quickly moved three lanes to my right and exited the freeway with flashing lights suddenly behind me. I would have tried to talk my way out of this ticket had Rooney not jumped into my lap and began mauling the window when the policeman's face appeared. I could only crack the window open far enough to slip my driver's license and registration through it, while Rooney carried on with his usual malephobic ruckus.

I realized Rooney was too smart for his own good when I was in my bank and he came strutting in to get me. He had figured out how to unzip the windows of the soft top on my jeep and had now become an escape artist. I sold my jeep and bought a "Rooney-proof" Bronco just for him.

Rooney's determination and mischievousness reminded me so much of myself that everyone, including me, began calling him my son. It was Rooney who taught Buster how to play and constantly made us all laugh. Rooney's powerful presence created an environment where no one around him could ever again be depressed, and so it has been ever since.

As I watched these dogs help each other overcome fears and obstacles, regaining the will to live, I knew I had been blessed and sent down the right road. I was driven to learn how to rehabilitate the "unadoptables," bringing out the best in each of them.

Snickers waving on command for
photo shoot

Snickers developed an impressive acting career. Skooter and Rooney made their TV debuts. Buster graduated from obedience class with a trophy and was too busy romping with the others and protecting "his" house to sleep much. Inky watched over us all with the wisdom of knowing that she was put in my life to help me save those in need.

Seeing these faces at our Thanksgiving table that year gave me more fulfillment than I had ever known before in my life. I would hope that anyone looking for their canine soul mate would now consider that shy one hiding in the corner with the frightened eyes. Nothing in my life has ever been as gratifying as seeing an abused or depressed dog lift up his head, look into my eyes, and wag his tail for the first time. Every day that happens becomes another day that I give thanks for all I've been given.

A Thanksgiving to remember

CHAPTER 5

GOOSE'S STORY
September 9, 1991

E very once in a while I believe we get a strong message from
above, telling us we're either still on the right path or to move
on to something else. I had such a message handed to me on a
very special day that has stayed with me forever.

Before Christmas, I went "pound hopping," looking for the right
pair of eyes to grab my heart and ask me to save its life. The urge hit
me to stop by Pet Adoption Fund and visit some of my new two-and
four-legged friends.

As busy as Pet Adoption Fund constantly seemed to be, one woman who worked there, Pat, always had such an inviting smile on her face
that I gravitated to her for help every time I visited. I suppose to some of
the other people working there I may have seemed like a pest. I always
had a million and ten questions about all of their dogs. But Pat always
stopped whatever she was doing so that she could help me, and that
made her irreplaceable in my eyes.

"Is there anyone in particular you want me to meet?" I asked her.

"No one in particular I can recall, Randi, but please go and walk through and meet everyone new."

Working at a busy rescue organization that held about two hundred dogs, with people abandoning them outside, even tying them to poles, must have been anything but harmonious and peaceful. It was beyond me how Pat was always calm, collected and gracious when dealing with the public.

I still felt a rush of adrenaline filling my body every time I approached a shelter or rescue facility. The seven-year-old girl in me never did die, and I felt as if I was in a candy store on my birthday when I was around masses of dogs needing homes. I bounced off to go look through all of the dog runs and ended up in one of the rooms filled with adorable smallish dogs. My eyes instantly locked with a very withdrawn, scraggly Scottish terrier mix, who looked as if he would have preferred to go unnoticed. I knew this was the one. He sat in the back of his cage, never moving or making a sound, while the other dogs pawed and barked for attention.

I rushed to get Pat and had her follow me back to this little dog's cage.

"He seems so scared. What do you know about him?" I asked her.

"Oh, that's Clancy. He's been here forever," she said. "His whole litter of puppies came here years ago. They were rescued from some crazy man in an apartment who was kicking them. The rest were adopted over three years ago, and all of them were very shy. Clancy was one of the worst and never got over it. You can't take him out. He's too scared and won't walk on a leash or let you hold him."

Pat was swamped with work and went back to the office to answer the phones. As usual, I didn't listen, and as soon as she was out of sight, I slowly cracked opened Clancy's cage to see if I could pet him. He was petrified but didn't snap at me or show any form of aggression. I instinctively knew that this was an incredible dog who deserved one day to associate humans with joy, not pain.

When I asked Pat if I could take him home, she almost collapsed and said, "Are you kidding? No one has ever even looked at Clancy. You know he has no training?"

"I don't care," I said. "I have to get him out of here, or I will never be able to sleep thinking about him."

Pat was overjoyed as she watched me load Clancy, stiff as a board in fear, into my truck and take him away from the only place he had known as home for most of his entire life.

My four-legged family seemed to know that Clancy needed them. With wagging tails, they gently welcomed him to our home of rehabilitation.

I thought I had experienced it all with regard to abused dogs, but Clancy showed me I was not finished learning. After being with him for over a month, it still took me about an hour to catch him in my yard, even with a leash dragging off him. He spent most of his time running away from me. He loved other dogs but hadn't improved in trusting humans. He still jumped away and stiffened up when I would catch him and corner him to pet him.

Just before Christmas, I found an amazing home for Clancy, where he had two canine sisters, one who had also been severely abused, and parents who were very understanding of his special needs.

Christmas passed and I again returned to Pet Adoption Fund to visit Pat and all of the new canine residents. When Pat saw me getting out of my truck, she immediately came up to me smiling.

"Oh, Randi, you know what? I forgot that Clancy has a brother who is still here. He was out being groomed the day you took Clancy home. Do you think you can take him? He'll never get adopted from here."

I picked out Clancy's brother, Kelsey, immediately from the two hundred other dogs. He was Clancy's clone—a dark gray, scraggly, short-legged terrier—only he was even more overtly fearful. As a puppy, his jaw had been dislocated and one of his eyes had been punctured. Now he pinned himself to the back of his cage and would sit up and beg to try to distance himself more from me. As I slowly tried to pet him, he gently pushed my hand away from his face with his paw as though he expected me to hurt him. His terror wrenched my heart, and I prayed I would forget that Kelsey's only chance at life outside that cage was through me. Unfortunately, this was a busy time in my life, with too many rescued dogs, and I was in no position to take on a hard case like Kelsey. Nevertheless, I visited him over the months and promised him I would bring him home before my birthday.

Finally, nearly four years since Kelsey had come to Pet Adoption Fund, he was freed from spending the rest of his life in a cage. I ecstatically brought him home.

My four-legged family knew also to treat him gently. But just three hours after Kelsey was with me, a neighbor opened my gate, and he was gone. My other dogs knew to stay at home, but Kelsey didn't even know where home was.

I searched for him through most of the night, then again when the sun rose, and put up flyers. But deep in my heart, I knew that no one could ever catch Kelsey. I had already put ID tags on him, but realized that no one would ever be able to get close enough to him to read them. My heart ached over the grim fact that Kelsey's first taste of freedom had to end this tragically. After a two-hour search the following afternoon, the call came.

"Hi, we have your dog. He was running on Ventura Boulevard near Balboa and crossing back and forth in between a lot of cars. Three of us chased him for forty-five minutes. Where do you live? We can bring him to you. He's really scared," the young woman's voice on the other end of the phone reported to me.

I had no idea who these people were, but I had already fallen in love with them. Kelsey was miraculously returned to me undamaged, at least physically. It had never been so clear to me that some angels were wrapped in human packages to watch over those in need. I padlocked all of my gates and felt both Kelsey and I were given second chances.

Kelsey continued to be horribly fearful and would not take food by hand or eat when any humans could see him. He did seem to like being with a pack of dogs and would often hide behind one of them when my mom or I came near him. He was one of the most innocent, gentle, and kind dogs I had ever known.

Never having been in a home as an adult dog, Kelsey had very few socialization skills and thought he was supposed to urinate in his food bowl. My mom instantly took to this one and defended his every move by saying things such as, "Look at how smart he is! He knew that he would have to sit in his urine when he was in a cage so he learned to go in his food bowl. He might even be smarter than Skooter-Boo 200 IQ." She soon claimed him as her dog, although he was no less terrified of her than anyone else.

My mom began telling Kelsey inflated tales of what an evil person I was, hoping to manipulate him into bonding with her. One day, I heard her talking to him from her bedroom.

"Now you really need to stay away from that mean lady. She will poke you with pins and scoop your eyeballs out with spoons if you get too close to her."

What she was referring to was the fact that I was the only one who would ever brush him or clean out his eyes, and no, I did not use pins or spoons. To my mom, all of these things were unnecessary and abusive to any dog, especially her Kelsey. Eventually, Kelsey began to believe her and would not leave her side. I became the "the mean lady," and she sang "his" song—"Someone to Watch Over Me"—to him every morning when he would awaken and look up at her with his big, terrified eyes.

My mom lived for Kelsey, and loved it when he would run to her to escape the imminent danger I imposed upon him any time I looked at him with amorous eyes. He was incredibly desirable and proved the old saying to be true: you always love what you can't have. Most of my volunteers and friends had insatiable appetites for being in Kelsey's presence. Everyone yearned to hold him or even touch him, but he would have nothing of it—except with my mom.

The horror stories that my mom told Kelsey of my wickedness grew larger by the day. She noticed he would now follow me around the house, and feared him opening up to people other than her. But the instant I would turn around to acknowledge him, he would scurry away and stumble into her arms, where she would tell him, "See, I told you so. She is evil. You need to stay away from her."

It was incomprehensible to me that my mom was actually an attorney. In some ways it seemed that, at least emotionally, she never developed past the age of eight.

The love affair between my mom and Kelsey continued, and he was even given his own voice so that he could carry on to the other dogs about my illicit plans to do away with him.

I have to admit that I was the one who gave the dogs their voices. I still believed as I did when I was at the shelter on my seventh birthday: "They all have so many interesting things to say to me." And I needed to speak for them in their different voices so that they could fully express

Goose cuddling up with brothers

themselves. Okay, maybe I shouldn't be judging my mom. I am probably more similar to her than I would choose to admit.

So, while I was creating Kelsey's voice, I realized that he would talk a bit funny if he ever did begin to talk, and this resulted in him acquiring a new name. Due to his dislocated jaw as a puppy, he had a lower front tooth that sat askew out of his scraggly, bearded face. Because of that, he would not have been able to pronounce Kelsey properly and could only say, "Kooshy," which eventually turned into "Goose."

My mom became overly protective of her Goose and convinced him that if she left him alone with me, his days would be filled with torture. She now began working from home to save him from me. Goose was so innocent and trusting of her that she talked him into believing that all other humans were evil too. He spent most of his time bustling to get away from everyone until they would ignore him, at which time he would turn around and begin to follow them. This became a game, and no one was quite sure if he really was frightened, or my mom had just brainwashed him into believing he should avoid everyone but her.

Having spent his life at a kennel, everything outdoors was wondrous for Goose. As long as the other dogs were with him and no humans were around, he loved investigating new things. The rain was beyond intriguing to him. He would sit outside and stare up at it for hours, and then rush into the house falling into my mom's arms saying, "Look, Mommy! The upside-down sprinklers are on again." Also, many a night I would have to drag him inside because he would sit in front of our hose, barking endlessly at it. Mom defended him: "Isn't he smart? The hose looks like a burglar hunched over, hiding in the bushes. Goose is protecting us. What would we do without him?"

My mom was in her own world of bliss with Goose, and he finally, occasionally, let me give him a bit of love too. But one day, all of that disappeared, when a small disaster struck our house.

I left my dogs for a little over an hour while I went to go bathe two of my new rescues. My mom was spending one of her rare days at her outside office.

When I returned, I wasn't quite sure what had happened, but the windows to the front of our house had somehow been opened, a hose had been stuck in the window, and some of the dogs were missing. The dogs who had stayed at home were drenched with water, and Buster, who was still too terrified to leave the house on his own, was sitting on our porch, dripping with water and pressed against the front door. Apparently, our house had been vandalized.

I heard my phone ringing and, when I answered it, the voice of a young boy said, "Hi, is your dog missing? We have him here at our house."

I hadn't yet figured out who was missing and I rushed down my street to the address the boy gave me. When I rang the doorbell, a woman led me into the living room where a family was embracing one of my adoption dogs, Chester Chedder Cheese.

Chester was a squatty, proud, briard mix to whom I was becoming far too attached, believing that no home would be good enough for his highness. This entire family was beaming, hugging Chester. It looked like a Kodak moment when the mom said, "We were hoping we wouldn't find his owners. Our dog died six months ago, and we have been waiting for the right one to come to us. We already love this funny guy, and we haven't even known him for an hour."

"Actually, I run a dog rescue agency, and Chester Chedder Cheese also stole my heart away with his charisma. I try to not get too attached to my rescues, but once in a rare while I can't help it. For the right family, and especially a close neighbor, he is available for adoption."

The entire family began hugging each other, while the kids jumped up and down arguing over who would get to sleep with Chester. I was hoping that this was the fairy tale ending to what appeared to be a minor disaster.

When I went back to my house to retrieve Chester's paperwork for his new family, I found that all of the other dogs were home...except for our Goose.

I instantly felt the life being sucked out of me and, for the first time in four years, believed this was a sign telling me that I was no longer meant to be rescuing dogs. I knew there was no way that Goose would be found a second time. As painful as it was, I had to face the reality of him living out his life on the streets or being hit by a car. I called my mom to tell her what had happened, and she was completely silent. She immediately left her office and came home.

Once again, I spent sleepless nights searching the streets and praying to anyone watching over us. I put up more flyers and asked people

The charming Chester Chedder Cheese

in my area if they had seen a little scraggly, scared gray dog. I placed ads in our local newspapers and spent the next few days crying for this little boy whose fate on earth was nothing but fear, pain, and suffering.

I had hoped that people who may have seen Goose over the weekend would have had more time to phone and let us know where he might have been. But the weekend passed, and he now had been missing for almost an entire week. I did not have the courage to call the Sanitation Department to see if Goose had been found dead on the street.

It was Monday, September the ninth, and a close friend who volunteered at Pet Orphans Fund, Tina Ladd, joined me to search the animal shelters one more time as we both truly felt that was where Goose would be. Tina was one of Goose's many secret admirers and tried to comfort me. "Don't worry, Randi. I know he will come back to us. We can't lose hope." But after visiting the two shelters closest to us, there was no sign of Goose and no "found reports" filed for any dog who could have resembled him. We left the shelter, slowly searching the streets, now unable to fight off our hopelessness.

We spent several more hours surveying the San Fernando Valley and finally returned to my home. I picked up my phone messages, which immediately brought tears to my eyes. Three messages had been left about Goose. Two of them were from people who had seen Goose running onto the freeway against traffic. The other message was from an elderly woman who said, "I'm so sorry about your dog. An entire group of people from an apartment complex overlooking the freeway tried to save him. I have him on my patio and will hold him until you can come for him."

I phoned back the woman, asking for her address, and rushed to her apartment. She walked me through her house and out to her patio where she again apologized. After running on the streets for almost a week and onto the very busy Ventura Freeway against traffic, my Goose was on her patio. She continued to apologize over the fact that he was tattered beyond belief—matted and covered from head to tail in burrs and foxtails.

Nothing gave me greater pleasure than being able to tell this woman Goose's story and the almighty miracle that had just occurred. I craved to hold Goose's little stocky body one more time. I yearned for him to

Randi and the elusive Goose

come back to me alive and healthy so that I could finish teaching him people can be trusted and really are not evil.

On September the ninth, my wishes were granted. On September the ninth, I was shown that I am doing what I'm supposed to be doing with my life. And on this spectacular day, September the ninth, 1991, I rejoiced in receiving a most sacred gift—Goose was given back to me on my twenty-ninth birthday.

CHAPTER 6

GIDGET'S STORY
November 24, 1991

Vinnie left a message in a weak, soft tone of voice that remains unforgettable. "I desperately need your help. I have to find a home for my Lhasa apso, Gidget. I love her so much, but I can't take care of her anymore. I don't have a choice. My health is failing. Please call me back."

As he sounded fairly young, I was confused, but returned his call. Since I am unable to help everyone who calls, I have to thoroughly screen each caller and then choose the ones I feel compelled to assist. Vinnie's was such a call.

Vinnie was in the advanced stages of AIDS. His medication was causing him to forget whether he had fed his dog, Gidget. It was also causing him to treat her in ways he never could have comprehended before he became so ill. Our conversation continued with Vinnie spilling out his guts to me. "Most of my friends have already died, and I've been relying on PAWS-L.A. to help me with Gidget. Have you heard of them? It's an organization that helps people with AIDS care for their pets, but it doesn't take them."

"Yes, I know about it. It's a wonderful organization," I quietly responded.

Vinnie continued, "They have been sending people here to walk Gidget several times a week, but that's not enough anymore. Most of my days are now spent at doctors' appointments, and I come home so exhausted that I sometimes am even resenting Gidget. My apartment is so small, and she's always underfoot, wanting attention. She needs to be walked several times a day to go to the bathroom, and I can't even do that. I can barely take care of myself. I spent every waking and sleeping moment of her life with her, and now I'm pushing her away in anger. It makes me so sad, but I don't have the energy to love her anymore."

"When would it be convenient for me to come? I can work my schedule around yours," I consoled the voice on the other end of the phone. This was one of those rare instances where time was no object for me, and I would not mention my unorthodox sleeping patterns.

"The sooner the better," he said. "I have to do this."

I had little knowledge of AIDS, but I immediately set an appointment to rescue Gidget from the hands of her once adoring, now tired owner. I was nervous and unsure about our meeting. Could I catch AIDS from something in his apartment or, worse, from his dog? What if he unconsciously became hostile toward me? I felt as alone in this rescue as Vinnie now felt in his life but knew I needed to hold my strength and face this situation.

The night before our meeting was yet another sleepless one for me with hundreds of worrisome thoughts not only for myself but for the loss that Vinnie would be experiencing.

When I arrived that next morning, I was relieved to see a very peaceful, calm, and gentle man. But the only recollection I had ever had of a body being this emaciated was from photos I had seen of Auschwitz survivors at the end of World War II.

Vinnie politely greeted me with the feeblest handshake I had ever felt. "Thank you so much for coming. I didn't know what I was going to do. No one else could help me."

"It's okay. I love being able to help," I solemnly replied.

As I slowly walked into his apartment, I noticed that it seemed to have been stripped of any items that would have made it feel like a home. One tattered, brown, cloth armchair stood alone in the corner of the naked living room. Gidget waddled up to me from behind it as though we were long-lost friends. Her unconditionally loving spirit felt like the only life remaining in Vinnie's apartment. Gidget had clearly forgiven her master for any ill treatment he may have unconsciously cast upon her. She was beaming with joy, following his every move.

Vinnie was barely able to walk me into his kitchen where he attempted to hand me the small bag of dog kibble that his frail body was unable to lift. I remained composed with a smile for his sake, but inside I was uncontrollably sobbing. Our meeting was brief and cordial, but I felt as though I was ripping the last remaining connection to life from someone who was nothing more than a victim to this dreadful epidemic. All the fear I had was now replaced with empathy.

I almost couldn't bear to watch Vinnie say good-bye to Gidget. When I picked her up to leave, he put his hand on my shoulder as if to stop me, but instead, he hugged me, cupped his trembling hands around Gidget's face and whispered to her, "Good-bye, my baby. Have a good life."

Holding back my tears, I left carrying Gidget and the dog kibble in my arms. I knew that Vinnie had no other reason to hold on to life now; he could let go. And although I knew that this rescue needed to happen, a part of me felt so criminal in doing so.

Gidget seemed to take this all in stride, maintaining her cheerful, loving personality. I was unable to tell Vinnie that Gidget would be very difficult for me to place as she was quite overweight and had a face that most would reject with an extreme underbite, tongue permanently hanging out, and big protruding eyes. Although I always prefer those with beautiful temperaments, unfortunately the general public disagrees and judges by appearances. I accepted that Gidget might live out her life with me. People either passed her by at my adoptions or commented on how funny looking she was. I maintained my hope that "her person" would enter her life.

One evening months later, I spoke with a very cheerful woman named Rosalind. When I answered the phone, my mood was uplifted by a giggly voice.

"Is this Randi?"

"Yes, it is. How can I help you?"

Rosalind's cheerfulness was contagious. After spending seven straight hours answering and returning phone calls, I would have been tired had any other voice been on the other end of the phone at 9:30 p.m.

"I'm looking for a little dog whose personality is like mine. Personality is number one."

My mind went into hyperdrive as I asked, "Do you have a preference for any breed, look, or age?"

"Well, I wouldn't want it to die on me right away, but other than that, no, as long as it is a happy, outgoing, little dog."

Many people who came to me to adopt a dog were very particular about the age, breed, color, and so on.

But Rosalind had a strong connection with God, and I suspected she would not judge those traits that Gidget was given by our Great Creator the way most other people had. When I described my bouncy, pudgy little Gidget to Rosalind, she bellowed, "She sounds just like me! When can I meet her? I'm so excited!"

I was even more excited and asked, "Can you come to my adoptions this Saturday? I'll be at the Petco in Studio City at 1 p.m. Gidget will be freshly groomed, cologned, and covered in bows, awaiting your arrival."

"I'll see you this Saturday!" Rosalind enthusiastically said.

That following Saturday as I was setting up puppy pens and unloading all of my rescued dogs, I could feel Rosalind's energy from a block away on Ventura Boulevard. I knew it was she because she exuberantly rushed right past all of us and began chuckling with joy when her eyes met Gidget's. Rosalind immediately dropped to the ground, embracing Gidget's perfection with the biggest of hugs. As a small group of us volunteers watched the two interacting with one another, it was unanimous—this match was most definitely made in heaven.

Gidget was Rosalind's dream come true, the one for which she had been searching.

Gidget started her new life just as her previous owner, Vinnie, ended his. I wished he could know the joy he left behind. I pray he is experiencing that joy now.

Rosalind and Gidget...A match
made in heaven!

CHAPTER 7

COCO'S STORY—A
BREEDER'S VALENTINE
February 14, 1992

When I awoke this Valentine's Day, giving gratitude for all of the loves in my life, the last thing I expected was to end the day with my heart crushed in a way it had never before known.

I had now been granted the reputation as "the savior of smallish mutts." But when Coco's parents phoned me for help, I couldn't turn them away.

"Randi? We don't know if you can help us but our vet recommended you. We were at a dog show three years ago and fell in love with the beauty of briards. One of the breeders at the show had a litter of puppies, and a thousand dollars later, we went home with one. Unfortunately, no one told us how protective they are. The breeder, who was also a vet, failed to inform us about the nature of briards. We recently contacted her, but she said that she is not breeding anymore and couldn't help us.

"Coco is a magnificent, gorgeous boy, who house-trained quickly, is obedience trained, and is the most loyal dog in the world. But we have one baby, another on the way, and we're getting very concerned about his protective growling."

I jumped in: "Is he neutered?"

"Well, our vet wasn't sure if it would make that much of a difference so we never did neuter him," Coco's mom responded. "What do you think?"

"It certainly can't hurt. It may help, and most important, whether or not you keep him, it will significantly reduce his chances of some forms of cancers," I informed her.

"Do you think it could stop him from biting again?" she asked.

"Wait—has he bitten and actually broken skin?" I abruptly asked, now determined to get to the whole story as quickly as possible.

To me, if skin hasn't been broken, the bite doesn't count. If a dog is truly aggressive and wants to hurt someone, it will. A warning "nip" is allowed as long as the dog's guardians are aware that the dog probably shouldn't be around children. I see too many people giving up on their four-legged "kids" just because they may growl over food or toys. Some dogs are just like spoiled children and don't like to share.

"Well, there was one small biting incident where he did break skin, but he was only protecting his house from our friends," Coco's mom defended him.

I could hear Coco's dad in the background also defending him.

These people really were lovely, and I could feel that they did not want to give up Coco. But briards are not known to be the best with kids, especially infants and toddlers. I had to be honest with them.

"Get him neutered," I told them, "as soon as possible and let me know how he's doing. It takes about six weeks for the hormones to change. If there will be a difference in his temperament, you may start to notice it after that time. If you do keep him, could you keep him separate from your kids?"

"He's used to having free run of our house. But our housekeeper is very concerned that he may hurt a child. I don't know what to do. Maybe you should begin looking for a new home for him," Coco's mom said in a defeated tone of voice.

"You really need to be sure of this before I start advertising him and screening potential new parents. He definitely should not be around kids at all, and if we do place him, he should only go to someone who is familiar with this or similar breeds. Are you sure you're ready to do this?" I asked.

"Yes," Coco's mom said. "My husband will have a more difficult time dealing with it. He's the one who obedience trained him, and Coco loves him to the bone. What should we do next?"

"Set up an appointment to get him neutered. I would love to meet him before advertising him. Can you bring him past Martex Pet Shop in Encino this Saturday after 1 p.m.?" I asked.

"Yes," she replied. "We'll have him groomed before then. We get him groomed about once a month. Oh, and Randi, he only growls some of the time. He really is a good dog. You will probably want to keep him for yourself."

I didn't think it was necessary to tell Coco's mom that I see thousands of dogs needing homes each year. I would never keep a young, beautiful, healthy purebred. I've always preferred the depressed or abused dogs, seniors, or funny-looking mutts who look as if they fell out of a cartoon or comic strip and have mismatched body parts. I never rescue a dog thinking I'm going to keep it. I would have hundreds living with me if I didn't make a diligent effort to place every dog I rescue.

But placing a large dog such as Coco, who had already bitten and was showing aggressive tendencies, would be no small feat. Before I would do anything with him, I would temperament-test him myself since I never take another person's word at face value when it comes to dogs.

I once had a woman bring me her dog of five years that she needed to place because she was moving. She told me that it was a Yorkshire terrier and weighed about ten pounds. Fortunately, I had over forty people waiting to adopt this breed, so I agreed immediately to help her and take the dog.

When a woman came walking up to my house with a bearded, sixty-five-pound shepherd mix, I thought she was visiting a neighbor and had gone to the wrong address. When I answered the door, I'm sure I looked confused when this woman acted as if she knew me and said, "Hi, Randi. I'm sorry I'm a little early."

I stared at her and then her sixty-five-pound bearded shepherd mix and said, "Oh my God! Who told you your dog was a Yorkshire terrier?"

"My vet," she naively replied.

"Is your vet sighted?" I asked. "Does he have a scale at his office? Your dog is as far from a Yorkie, or even a mix of the breed, as you can get. If anything, she is an Airedale mix."

Unfortunately, at that moment, none of the people who were anxiously awaiting this ten-pound Yorkshire terrier were interested in adopting a sixty-five-pound shepherd mix. Rarely does guilt overcome me, but this woman truly believed that her beloved dog of five years was a ten-pound Yorkshire terrier. I felt awful turning her away and offered to help her place her shepherd mix, but at that time, I had no foster homes for a dog of this size or anyone waiting to adopt a cute, large dog like this.

After that fiasco, I learned never to take a person's word at face value, especially over the phone.

So, I wasn't quite sure what to expect on Saturday at my adoptions. But when everyone's heads turned toward a magnificent, handsome, well-behaved, pure-bred, tawny-colored briard, who was prancing toward us like a Lipizzan show horse, heeling next to his dad like an obedience champion, I was overjoyed. Coco was stopping traffic with his striking looks and people came rushing over to us from blocks away, eager to touch him. I was concerned that he might snap, bite, growl, or show some other sign of protectiveness. But Coco was as well mannered as a dog could be.

I couldn't believe that Coco was the same dog that his parents had described to me, and said, "Wow! He's way too perfect for me ever to consider keeping him. I bet we'll have a bunch of people wanting to adopt him. Are you still sure you want to do this?"

Coco's dad could barely look me in the eyes and replied, "I think we really have to. He is very protective at home, and my wife is so worried with the new baby on the way. We're getting him neutered next week."

I placed ads and found prospective owners who knew about briards, but Coco's parents, after neutering him upon my request, decided that they couldn't part with him. They hoped the neutering would stop his aggressiveness.

About a month later, Coco's mom, who believed they now had a lawsuit against them, contacted me again. Coco had bitten their babysitter while she was picking up their baby. Again, this is not abnormal briard behavior, and Coco did what he thought he was supposed to do.

Coco's mom pleaded with me: "Randi, I'm so afraid we may lose our house over this. He bit our babysitter very badly. We really need your help now."

I again began advertising Coco, screening through all interested parties while disclosing his past. Many people were still interested in adopting this gorgeous boy, and I ended up placing Coco in a home with a lady who knew the breed and had no children. This was ideal. She lived on two acres with horses and welcomed his protectiveness. But, the next day, she returned Coco for growling at her most of the twenty-four hours that she kept him.

Whenever I place a dog, the new owners sign a contract agreeing to abide by certain rules. In turn, Recycled Pets takes its dogs back or re-homes any of its dogs for the rest of that animal's lifetime. I never want any of our dogs to end up in a shelter or in a home where it is no longer loved or wanted.

I placed more ads and had well-behaved Coco at one of my adoptions where over ten people wanted this lovable beauty. Understanding now that Coco preferred men, I searched again for the perfect home. I found a single, tall, dark man whose gruff voice I was sure Coco would respect. This man had had a Great Dane who shared his bed and limousine until the Dane died of old age. I was ecstatic when he said he knew about briards and their protectiveness. Coco loved this man when they met, and I could see that this time it was definitely going to work.

We spoke almost daily as I received updates on their bonding. The new dad reported to me, "Coco's growling isn't really bothering me 'cause I know it's gonna take time for him to get used to me. But I don't know why he keeps goin' off on his own to sit in the corner, where he keeps banging his head up against the wall. Do you know anything about that or why a dog would do somethin' like that?"

I couldn't pretend to know the answer to any behavior like that, and Coco's original parents never mentioned such a thing to me. Nonetheless, Coco's new dad was already enamored with him and took him everywhere he went in his limousine. They were inseparable.

I hadn't heard from Coco's new dad for over a week. Then he phoned to say, "I'm sorry, Randi. I gave it my best shot, but I can't live in fear of my life anymore. I need to return him to you."

I had no idea what he was talking about but realized that he had been under-reacting to the behaviors when he told me this final incident.

"The two of us got up in the morning and were both doin' our thing. I walked into the living room where Coco was standing very still, and then he began staring at me. Then, all eighty pounds of him started growling at me. There was nothin' he was protecting. Nothin' or no one. I did what you said and gruffly corrected him with a 'NO.' But Coco growled even more ferociously and wouldn't stop staring me down. Then he slowly began moving toward me growling harder. I didn't know what to do, so I turned to get my gun in the kitchen. When I turned back around, Coco lunged onto me—and with his tail wagging, began kissing me. Man! I didn't know what the hell that was all about. But I was scared, and nothin' scares me!

"Later that day he went after me again in my car, and I got away from him, but I think there's somethin' really wrong with him. Somethin's not firing right upstairs."

I planned to meet Coco's very patient, newest dad at a shelter where a friend of mine was volunteering. I made many phone calls to breeders, vets, other rescues, and even some of my own volunteers, asking for suggestions. Everyone unanimously agreed that Coco was nothing but a liability. None of the briard rescues would take him, and no one was willing to help me in any way with him. My friend was going to support me in the follow-through of this inevitable "dirty deed."

I felt as though I had failed and was putting one of my own three-year-old healthy dogs to sleep. I was nauseated. In almost five years of rescuing hundreds of dogs, I never had to have one euthanized, and it went against my belief system.

As I was leaving for the shelter, another friend who had adopted a dog from me called after hearing about this and tried to talk me out of putting Coco to sleep. But she had never met him and was also unwilling to help me with him. Now the thought of putting Coco to sleep was again even more incomprehensible to me.

As Coco came up to me at the animal shelter, putting his big fluffy paws on my shoulders while kissing me, I looked into his beautiful eyes, and I just couldn't bring myself to do it. What can I say? I was a sucker for a pretty face. Even the man Coco had terrorized for the last few weeks couldn't leave. He sat with Coco and me at the shelter while I desperately made more phone calls in an attempt to save his life.

All of the volunteers and kennel workers kept saying, "Are you crazy, Randi? This dog is a lawsuit waiting to happen."

I wasn't sure what I was going to do with this gentle giant who showed only love and proper manners the entire day I was with him. People visiting the shelter were admiring Coco all day long and he never growled or showed any signs of aggression. I did everything possible to see the other side of Coco that I had only heard about, but he just wagged his tail while cuddling and remained a perfect gentleman.

As the shelter was closing, my prayers were answered. I found a foster home for Coco with a couple who had recently adopted another dog from me. For safety's sake, based on what I was told but had yet to see, they agreed to keep a muzzle on Coco until we were sure it would be safe to do otherwise, removing it only for him to eat or drink.

I hesitantly put the muzzle on Coco before loading him into my truck to deliver him, as I recalled his supposed unstable car behavior. He was completely submissive and again a perfect gentleman. I prayed to God that I had made the right decision. I truly felt there was someone out there for him who knew and owned briards, appreciating all of their quirks. I told myself, "Maybe all the people who had him didn't know what they were doing. He was fine with me and responded to my corrections and commands."

I was feeling even more right about my decision as I kept seeing his gorgeous, gentle face in my rearview mirror. I spoke to him, while driving, "Please tell me what you want, Coco. I know everyone is saying I should put you to sleep, but I really don't want to. Please prove all of these people wrong for me."

I needed to see it myself. Sometimes people overreact and don't know dogs the way I do. I called Coco's original owners during the day, and his mom was very appreciative of my efforts to save his life, but understood if I needed to do otherwise. His first dad couldn't even discuss anything about him, as he was still severely mourning Coco's absence.

I even spoke to the woman who was Coco's breeder, and she said, in a raspy smoker's sounding voice, "Oh, he's just acting like a briard. Give him a little smack across the face, and he'll stop."

"But will you take him back?" I begged her. "No one seems to be able to understand him."

"Oh, honey, I don't do this anymore. You're on your own. Good luck," as she slammed down the phone.

I did indeed feel as if I was on my own while I was driving and seeing nothing but handsome Coco in my rearview mirror. I made one quick stop and kissed Coco as I left him in my truck for a few minutes. I was falling in love on this Valentine's Eve.

A few minutes later, I returned to my truck, excited to see Coco, and said, "Hi, my handsome," as I opened the door.

Had Coco not been muzzled, I have no idea what might have happened. He showed me his teeth as he growled while staring me down. I gruffly said, "No!" which caused him to become more aggressive. His eyes were now filled with rage, and nothing I could do would stop him. As he lunged toward me to attack, I quickly shut the door and left. For almost an hour, I tried to get back into my truck, but Coco seemed to act as if I was now his enemy, each time lunging at me to attack me.

Over an hour later, when I was able finally to creep back into my truck, ignoring Coco, I was crushed. Coco told me what he wanted.

I slowly drove back to the shelter hoping this wasn't true. I was now in fear of Coco.

The shelters are open twenty-four hours to receive animals, so even though it was after 7 p.m., I was able to bring Coco back. Everyone working at the shelter knew me and asked what had happened.

As I unmuzzled Coco with him kissing my face, tears began to form in my eyes. The words I could barely speak, "I am requesting to have Coco destroyed," still haunt me years later.

I hoped they would believe nothing was wrong with him, but it wasn't so. Two of the people working at the shelter said, "We really don't want to handle him, Randi. You'll have to walk him back to the euthanasia room yourself."

I walked Coco through the shelter, passing hundreds of homeless dogs, and stepped over the pile of unwanted canine carcasses in the euthanasia room. My body froze when I reached to open the cage to put Coco in it. I felt as if I was in the middle of a bad dream and was hoping someone would rescue me from it. I had to force myself to leave Coco in the small cage where he would spend his last night. The veterinary technician performing the euthanizing wouldn't be in until the morning.

I drove home that Valentine's eve with tears drowning my face. Coco's big, sensitive eyes kept flashing through my mind.

I sat outside until 6 a.m. writing Coco's story. The gentle wind and my own sweet dogs soothed my damaged heart.

And to Coco: I'm sorry. I tried.

In Memoriam
Coco

CHAPTER 8

THE DAY SAINT
FRANCIS SMILED
November 30, 1992

T he tears have been numerous throughout my dog-rescuing career. But tonight I'm singing, dancing, laughing, crying, and sharing this rapture with my very extended four-legged family. They experience it all with me. Tonight they know my tears are of joy, stemming from the culmination of the most magnificent twenty-four hours of rescue that I have ever known.

Most of the dogs I rescue are from animal shelters. Some, however, are dogs that other rescue organizations have not been able to place.

Casey and Oliver were mid-sized, curly-coated cockapoo brothers, who were very adoptable as puppies when they ended up at a private, no-kill rescue shelter. But for some reason, they were never adopted and spent the next four years of their lives together in a small room, waiting for a family that never arrived.

When I went into their room to sit with them, they both ran to the back corner, huddling against each other and staring at me, trembling. Four years of living in a private room at a kennel had made them terrified of everyone except for the workers who had fed them. It would be difficult enough to rehabilitate and place only one of them, but the thought of now taking them away from each other was worse than letting them live out their lives here.

I sat on the floor at the opposite side of their room and whispered to them in a soft, gentle tone of voice. "You boys don't even know how gorgeous you are. I bet people will be fighting over you soon enough. I can't take you home with me now—not that either of you look as though you want to leave your safe room and come with me—but I promise to show you a different life before the end of this year. You'll see. I promise to come back for you."

Casey and Oliver never took their enormous eyes off me, shaking the entire time I spoke softly to them.

With a huge demand from people now wanting to adopt dogs from my rescue agency, I spent the following months hustling from shelter to shelter, rescuing as many dogs as possible. Many of these discarded dogs were very adoptable with only a mini-makeover—a grooming, cologne, and bows on their collars, ears, or heads. But Casey and Oliver were always in the back of my mind as I continued rescuing and placing so many other dogs over the next several months. Their frozen, trembling bodies and enormous, horrified eyes continued to cry out to me louder by the day.

Honoring my commitment, I returned to Casey and Oliver's shelter to help them begin their new lives. The horror on their faces again broke my heart. Casey was the shier of the pair and defecated as I slowly approached them. It was then that I also noticed he had a rear club foot, making him even less adoptable. Oliver again just trembled while staring at me. I sat at the opposite end of their room, and after an hour of reassuring them, we were on our way home. Casey and Oliver sat pressed against each other like conjoined twins in the backseat of my truck and, for the first time in four years, saw life outside of the kennel.

I had arranged for a foster person to temporarily care for them, but as soon as she met the boys, she changed her mind.

What was I going to do with this fragile pair of brothers? As usual, I had many other dogs to work with and place in new homes. But I had no choice except to add Casey and Oliver to the group and bring them to my home. I felt it would be important to give them their own space during this transition period, so I kept them together at the

Casey and Oliver

opposite end of the house from where the other "recycled pets" were temporarily residing.

I often didn't truly appreciate the fact that my mom had allowed me to turn her house into Encino's only canine rehabilitation center, but realizing this passion must be genetic, I had always hoped she wouldn't notice. Now, with Casey and Oliver, it would be difficult to hide the truth that almost every room of our 2,500-square-foot house was graced with dog energy.

Several days later I was holding one of my open house adoptions and I looked forward to beginning the socialization of my new boys with the public. As I went into their private "suite," my mind pictured some of the many things to which I would now slowly be exposing them, all foreign to their four-year-old, sheltered eyes. Traveling in a truck with many other dogs, having strangers ogling them and attempting to pet them, and spending the day in a busy pet store could be very stressful for Casey and Oliver. I was prepared to bring them home early if necessary. When I approached Casey, he began to snap at me, and I was unable to get him to budge even an inch. Oliver, although looking at me as if I were a serial killer, was willing to let me handle him and, as I slipped a leash around his neck, trotted out to my truck with me. I decided to take him alone to my adoptions so that I could at least begin his road to recovery.

When I arrived at my adoptions without Casey, the consensus of my volunteers was never to let them see each other again. Everyone except me believed that they would never get adopted if I kept them together. My heart ached at the thought of separating them, and I feared that this might be their only chance at a new life.

Throughout the day, I was very impressed with the progress we all witnessed in Oliver's temperament. He was doing splendidly with many strangers staring at him and even allowed people to pet him without appearing as though he was convulsing in fear. I was so very proud of him and thrilled that several people even expressed an interest in adopting him. But I was not going to separate Oliver and Casey that quickly or easily. They were merely infants in their emotional evolution. Separating them would have seemed no different to me than taking puppies away from their mothers before they were weaned.

When I reunited Oliver with Casey that evening, they were so ecstatic that they seemed to forget I was a human they were supposed to fear, and by accident, both kissed me, while tangoing with each other.

Usually exhausted after a full day of Saturday adoptions, preceded by an all-nighter of grooming, my Sundays were reserved for an occasional private dog showing or simply returning phone calls. But this weekend, I was overly ambitious and eager to propel Casey and Oliver's rehabilitation. I decided to waive my day of rest and return to Petco on Sunday for another full day of adoptions.

While squeezing in a few morning phone calls—mostly from people wanting toy breed puppies, which rarely need rescuing—one call stood out.

"Hi, my name is Cathy. I have a nine-year-old son who is very gentle, but he has allergies. We've been wanting a dog for years, and I think it's a good time to start looking to adopt. We were told that poodles or mixes are good for people with allergies. I don't want to bring my son today, because he'll want to take all of the dogs home, and I don't want him to be let down if we don't find one. He's very sensitive."

As always, I began to ask some questions to get a better sense of what Cathy was like and the home situation.

"What is the oldest age you would be interested in adopting?" I asked.

"Well, I am a teacher and gone during some of the day, so I don't think a puppy or a young dog would suit us. We would love one that was already house trained, but we can work with the dog. Both my son and I are very patient."

I already adored Cathy and said, "If you can please come to meet some very special boys I will have at my adoptions at the Petco in Studio City after noon today, I will tell you the story behind both of them. I have to run now to get everything together for the adoptions, but I hope you can come. I would love to talk to you more."

The morning before an adoption event always challenged my multitasking skills. I usually wear a headset with a phone attached and have a dog under each arm while putting ID tags, collars, bows, and cologne on everyone. These were just the finishing touches. Many people commented that I always saved these things for the last minute and should have done this the night before. But the night before always included bathing everyone, haircut touch-ups, giving any last vaccinations, and preparing all of the adoption applications, contracts and paperwork for each dog. In my life, every minute felt like the last minute, and the twenty-four hours in each day never felt like enough time.

I often attempted to blame my rushing around and consistent tardiness on the many white dogs who would inevitably play in the mud the morning before an adoption after just being bathed. But the same excuse can only be used so often before people would eventually call my bluff. The truth is that I've always been most comfortable with this type of a hectic life, and I have no interest in trading it for anything else.

Those few energizing minutes talking with Cathy infused me with enough steam to make it through a second day of adoptions on very little sleep. I excitedly went to the other end of the house to tell Casey and Oliver about Cathy and to load them into my truck, but Casey again decided that we were not friends and began trembling so hard that he could not control his bodily functions. I could see that he would most definitely snap at me in fear if I tried to take him away from his safe haven. So I left him alone as his courageous brother, Oliver, once again followed me out of the room and into my truck.

When I arrived at my adoptions for the second time without Casey, I tried to ignore the comments I continued to hear such as "Randi, you really need to place Oliver on his own. He'll do fine without Casey. Look at how well he did yesterday at the adoptions. Casey really needs to be put to sleep. They'll never know the difference, and Casey's going to end up being a biter. At his age, he'll never get over his fear and anxiety." But I only saw a gentle, sweet, terrified little boy inside of Casey who, with time I believed, would overcome all of this. It seemed that I so often lacked patience with many things except for an abused or traumatized dog. The thought of putting Casey to sleep made me sick to my stomach, and I hoped I would continue to tune out most of the advice I was receiving.

I put a card next to Oliver that briefly told his story and the fact that his "other half" was unable to attend the adoptions "due to prior commitments." Several people who were interested in adopting Oliver tried to coax me into letting him go home with them that day, but I remained steadfast in my commitment to Casey and Oliver. Giving them a better life did not include separating them. Two of those people who were interested in adopting Oliver left, angry with me, and one man uttered under his breath, "This is supposed to be an adoption with dogs needing homes. What the hell are you doing here anyway if you won't let us take this dog?"

Through the cloud of negativity, a smiling, petite woman emerged, introducing herself as Cathy. Thank you, God! I told her the entire story and then broke the news to her that Oliver had a brother so frightened that I was unable to bring him.

"Oh, my gosh!" Cathy said, in her positive, uplifting voice. "That's wonderful! We were hoping to get a pair of dogs so that they could keep each other company. May I spend some time with Oliver and see if we connect?"

"Cathy, I don't know if you clearly understand. Oliver's brother, Casey, is so frightened that he's snapping when I approach him. I don't know if I would put him with a nine-year-old."

"Well, my son is very shy, not the type of child who would invade a dog's space if I warn him ahead of time. My only concern would be my son's allergies," Cathy said, caressing Oliver who was now sitting in her lap. "Oliver is delightful. With some time and patience, I can't imagine his brother would be a problem. Could we set up a time to have my son meet both of them?"

Cathy was more than willing to fill out my three-page adoption application, and as I expected, she received an A+.

"Cathy, you're a godsend," I said, very relieved. "I knew I needed to be here today and hold adoptions. I don't know if Casey and Oliver are ready to go to a home yet or if I'll even be able to transport both of them to your house. But I'm going to call you tonight to discuss it. As far as I'm concerned, they're spoken for, and my mission has been accomplished. I feel like I can go home now."

That night, Cathy and I spoke on the phone for over forty-five minutes, and we set a tentative time for me to attempt to bring Casey and Oliver to her house the following day at 5 p.m.

Most of the next day was consumed by rescuing more dogs out of the animal shelter in Ventura County, which was about forty-five minutes from my house. This shelter euthanized many dogs, who would be very desirable in my neck of the woods, and my Bronco drove there on autopilot at least once a week.

I barely had time to begin the task of transporting Casey and Oliver to their potential new home. Had I not been so busy, I'm sure I would have expended much energy worrying about Cathy finding another dog on this day or her son being bitten by Casey or them simply changing their minds. But there was no time for worrying on this day. I had a house full of new rescues and, before I knew it, I was giggling away with my favorite volunteer and friend, Sarah Belgard, as the two of us were attempting to lift a humongous crate with Casey and Oliver in it. The two of them were staring out of the crate at us as though we were both insane.

Sarah had come up with the brilliant idea of having Casey follow Oliver into an oversized crate filled with the most succulent dog snacks. She hid behind a door where they could not see her and quickly closed the crate door behind Casey as soon as he followed Oliver into it. Her plan worked. But both Sarah and I barely stand five feet, two inches tall, and we had the most awkward time of it, trying to carry this huge crate with over sixty pounds of trembling terrified dogs through my house, down some steps, into the garage, and up into the back of my Bronco. We didn't have time to fail at this; we were already running a bit late. I don't think we ever stopped laughing on the entire drive to Cathy's house and, when we arrived, were wondering how we would be able to reverse this process now that the adrenaline rush had worn off.

But when it came to helping an animal, Sarah's commitment and determination were, undying, and within minutes, Casey and Oliver were sitting in this huge crate in the middle of Cathy's living room. Her son was exactly as she had described him, gentle, calm, and respectful.

As Sarah opened the door to the crate, Casey and Oliver slowly emerged and began surveying their new surroundings. Sarah and I didn't have a moment even to consider how traumatic the transporting experience must have been for them. It appeared that our carefree and jovial attitude must have rubbed off on Casey and Oliver, because they also seemed to have forgotten their fears. Before we knew it, they were dancing throughout the house and yard together, with Cathy's well-behaved son following, allergy-free.

We stayed for over an hour watching this new family bond. It was clear to us all that this is where Casey and Oliver were meant to be. As we left, with tears rolling down our faces, Sarah and I knew that Someone from above had created this very special home for these very special boys.

After rushing home from Casey and Oliver's adoption, Sarah and I barely had time to catch our breath before tending to all of our newly rescued dogs from the Ventura County Animal Shelter.

I had a method to the madness of sorting through hundreds of dogs needing homes and selecting only a few that I would be able to rescue at any given time. I would make a list first of the dogs that were going to be put to sleep as the top priority to rescue. Next on my list were the dogs turned in by their owners, as they could be put to sleep at any time if the shelter became overcrowded or if those dogs became ill with parvo, distemper, or kennel cough. Then came the very adoptable, small, young, cute dogs, as those were the least at risk of being destroyed.

The morning of Casey and Oliver's adoption, I was in deep concentration, sorting through my paperwork of the dogs I was interested in rescuing at this shelter. The supervisor, Officer Worley, came up to me with a very serious look on her face and said, "Randi, when you have a minute, I need to talk to you." It seemed as if I was in trouble for something, so I immediately stopped what I was doing and followed her into her office. She began to tell me a story about a dog that they were trying to locate.

"We don't know if you may have rescued this particular terrier mix out of here about two months ago, but a man contacted us looking for his dog. Although he lives over two hours away, in Orange County, he is contacting every shelter in Southern California, hoping to find his dog. He went out of town and left his dog with a friend's mother, who was supposed to take care of it until he came back. But for some reason that no one can understand, she turned the dog into a shelter and won't tell him where. It's been over two months now and the man hasn't been able to find his dog. He fears it was put to sleep at a shelter. May I give him your phone number? You rescue so many dogs from here. Maybe it was one that you took out and placed."

My mind started to create horrid visions of some crazy man coming after me for rescuing and placing his dog, when Officer Worley must have picked up on my thoughts and interjected, "Randi, you're under no obligation to return the dog to him. If it was a dog that you took out of our shelter, you legally became the owner when you bailed him out of here. But even if you did rescue and place his dog, the man may find comfort in discovering that it was not destroyed."

"Are you sure it would be safe to give him my number?" I asked. "I wouldn't want him to be angry with me for any reason if it was one that I rescued and placed."

"Again, Randi, you are under no obligation to talk to him if you are not comfortable. It's up to you," Officer Worley said.

"Well, I guess you can give him my number. I don't mind talking to him."

I carried on with my dog selection process at the shelter and, two hours later, ecstatically drove home with my new rescues. Looking at the faces of the dogs whose lives I've just saved remains one of the biggest highs I've ever known. I had to train my mind not to look back at all of the faces I left behind. As with most everything, I was discovering how important it was for me consciously to choose thoughts that uplifted and invigorated me instead of the many negative ones I found myself always gravitating toward. The negative ones seemed to suck the life out of me. If I allowed my mind always to run rampant, I would not be able to survive my world of rescuing.

In a little less than an hour, I arrived at Martex Pet Shop in Encino, where the owners, Bill and Susan, opened their arms once again to my truck full of newly rescued dogs. They helped me carry them into the grooming room where the magnificent makeovers began.

I held one of my new dogs in my arms while I picked up over ten phone messages. I was baffled by one message that I could barely understand. I replayed it several times in an attempt to make out what was being said and realized that it was a distraught woman who was sobbing over the loss of her dog. I immediately phoned her back while Susan continued the grooming of the new rescues.

"Hi, this is Randi. I'm returning your call. Is this Chris?"

"Oh, Randi!" she said, instantly bursting into tears. "I got your name from the sh-sh-sh-shelter. I'm sorry. I can barely talk. My dog just died and I can't go on without her. I don't know what to do. I need to find her a-a-again. My family lived for her, and she was the best d-d-dog in the world. I need to come see you."

"Chris," I calmly said, trying to help her gain enough composure so that we could have a two-way conversation, "Chris, I don't know if I can help you. But maybe it would make you feel better just to come and hold some of my dogs." I slowly began to shed a tear with her as I could empathize with her pain. "Chris, when my dog Skippy died, I didn't think I could go on either. I started my rescue after going through that. It ended up being a blessing. Tell me about your little girl."

Again she could barely talk. I could hear that her face was flooding in tears when she said, "K-K-Kisses was a little tan dachshund-terrier mix. She was our baby. She had one ear that stood up and the other flopped down. She slept in bed with us, and she loved my husband Ga-Ga-Gary. He spoiled her so bad. I need a pu-pu-puppy just like her."

I couldn't believe what I had just heard. The dog I was holding in my arms was a little female dachshund-terrier mix that had been on the list to be put to sleep at the shelter that same day. I almost didn't take her because she was a bit homely and middle-aged. I thought it might take a long time to find someone to adopt her. She was a scraggly little girl with one ear that stood out in a funny way.

"Chris," I said, "I've never seen a litter of puppies exactly like Kisses. I don't know how you could even find a puppy exactly like her, but I have to tell you what I'm holding in my arms as we speak."

When I described this waif to Chris, she asked, sobbing even harder, "Randi, can I come right now? Where are you?"

When we hung up the phone and I told Susan the story, she grabbed this little girl from my arms and rushed her to the tub to bathe her. About an hour later, Chris walked into the grooming room and saw my scruffy new rescue sitting in a cage, drying, with her one ear pricked upright. Chris stumbled over herself while quickly reaching for her.

"Oh my God, Randi! I can't believe it!" She said, with her entire face red and her eyes swollen like water balloons. "This is a miracle. I know she may not act like Kisses, but I've never seen another dog so much like her. Lovie is your new name and you're coming home with me," Chris said to the little dog. "I don't care how you act, how old you are, or if you're even trained. You are meant to be mine."

Chris wasn't interested in waiting to bring a new dog home to grieve the loss of Kisses. Lovie's life was spared to help Chris heal quickly and to teach us all a bit more about faith.

Susan was almost finished grooming everyone when a woman stood in the doorway and politely poked her head in, saying, "Is Randi

Lovie

The little girl cocker spaniel,
soon to be named Precious

here? We've been speaking on the phone. I'm the one looking to adopt a female cocker spaniel."

I was now helping with the grooming and stopped to wipe off my wet hands on a towel and introduce myself. Even though I had no idea who this woman was, I reached out my hand and said, "Hi, I'm Randi."

I didn't remember talking to this woman, but I speak to so many new people every day that I often don't recall some of my conversations. I rarely rescue cocker spaniels, so I probably assumed that this woman went to one of the other rescues to which I refer people.

Many cocker spaniels that I saw in the shelters were very high-strung and were turned in for biting. I usually prefer to rescue the calm, older, depressed dogs that weren't bouncing off of the walls. Although I do love all dogs, I don't believe in cages and prefer not to have a house full of hyperactive dogs.

But rescuing dogs from an animal shelter is like picking a grab bag out of a barrel—you really don't know what you're getting. In an attempt to eliminate extra stress in my life, I always temperament-test any dog I consider taking and, on this amazing day, could not leave another particular dog behind who was also on the list to be destroyed.

This woman continued: "I phoned you several times in the last week. You said you might be here grooming the dogs that you were rescuing out of the shelter today, so I thought I would stop by. It's Rose—do you remember me?"

"Oh my God! I'm so sorry. I completely remember you now. Really, it's not early-onset Alzheimer's," I joked. "I have so much on my mind and talk to so many people every day, but we spoke quite a few times, right?"

"Yes," she said politely. "I've been searching for an older, calm female cocker. I know you said you rarely take them in, but I thought I would stop by and say hi anyway since I live so close. Susan used to groom my other cocker, who just died several months ago."

Susan turned from the grooming tub when she heard her name and, when she saw one of her devoted customers, bellowed, "Rose! How are you? You'll never believe what Randi just brought back from the shelter!"

Susan stepped aside from the dog she was finishing blow-drying to reveal the only cocker spaniel I had rescued in months. Rose put her hand up to her mouth in disbelief and said, "Oh, my gosh, is it a girl?"

"As girly as you can get," Susan said.

"Rose, this is the sweetest little girl cocker I've ever met. She was in the pound listed as a stray with no name and when I went into her cage to sit with her, I couldn't let her die. I know I told you I don't usually take cockers, but this one is exceptional. She's a doll, and both Susan and I already love her," I enthusiastically said.

Rose smiled and when she went up to this little nameless girl, received an immediate lick on her nose. Susan lifted the cocker out of the tub and put a collar and leash on her. She handed it to Rose, saying, "Why don't you take her for a walk?"

When the two returned about twenty minutes later, Rose knelt down, hugging the gentle little girl cocker and said, "Randi, I've been looking for months. She's exactly what I want. When can I have her?"

"Well," I said, "she's already been spayed and can go home any time. I can send you to my vet, who will give her a checkup if you would like."

"Can I have her today?" Rose excitedly asked. "I've been waiting so long to be some little girl's mother again."

I followed Rose and her new daughter to her house, filled out all of the adoption paperwork with them, and went back to Martex feeling as if I was floating on a cloud. This day in the life of dog rescue was already an unprecedented one.

Susan offered to watch my other rescues while I rushed home to take Casey and Oliver to start their new life.

I again picked up my phone messages and thought I was in trouble for something when I heard a confusing message from a serious-sounding man who almost seemed angry. I immediately returned his call, and he frantically began reciting a very long story about the last three months of his life.

Steven's words seemed convoluted because he was deeply depressed. His story ended with: "Anyway, I was given your number by the shelter in Ventura County. You are my last hope. I've searched through every other shelter with no luck. I just sat at Thanksgiving dinner more melancholy than ever before in my life, feeling like I would never know what happened to my dog. My friend's mother, I think, went off the deep end. We have no idea why she may have turned my dog into a shelter after agreeing to watch him for me. She will not tell me where she took him."

"Steven, I'm so sorry, but after two or three months he could be anywhere in Southern California if he did end up getting adopted from a shelter. I take so many terrier mixes from the shelters that I probably wouldn't even know if I had rescued your dog. What was he like?"

"I watched Putty being born four years ago," Steven said. "We went to obedience classes where he won first place, and I trained him to do many different tricks. He's so smart. I never want to go through another Thanksgiving like this, wondering what happened to him."

"Well, I haven't rescued any dogs who would fit into that 'well-trained Einstein category' in the last few months," I said, "but what did he look like?"

"Putty is the most handsome wire-haired terrier mix you've ever seen," his proud father replied.

"Did he have any characteristics that would set him apart from other cute terrier mixes?"

"Aside from him being the most handsome dog you've ever laid eyes on, one of his eyes is brown and the other is blue. I picked him out of the litter because of that."

I honestly had not rescued any well-trained, incredibly handsome terrier mixes in the last several months, but I did have one dog with different colored eyes. The chances of it being this man's dog were close to zero. He lived in Orange County, about two hours from me, and another forty-five minutes from the Ventura County shelter. This dog was anything but handsome or smart. He was a gangly, unsocialized, sweet oaf that Sarah had named Gofer.

Gofer was one of my unadoptables, and everyone passed him by at my adoptions. He had become one of our own favorite adoption dogs because he always kept his chin up as he watched his other friends come and go. Oftentimes he would be the only one who would come home with me at the end of an adoption day.

This couldn't be Steven's dog anyway because our vet, who neutered him, said that he was only about one and a half years old, not four.

In the back of my mind, I was hoping Steven would come to meet Gofer anyway and possibly adopt him while he continued to search for Putty. Gofer would love a sibling. In the two-plus months he had been with me, he was constantly cheery, always befriending each new dog that came in and was adopted from my rescue.

When I told Steven about Gofer, he said, "Randi, would you mind doing me a favor? I know this isn't my dog, but would you just try something? I trained Putty to jump into my arms on command. I would put my arms out and say, 'Putty, up!' He would always jump right off the ground and into my arms."

"Steven, this dog Gofer is too big to jump into someone's arms. He's kind of long-legged and gangly. He would knock someone over."

"Randi, please just try it," he begged me.

Sarah had come over when I was on the phone with Steven, and I told him to hold on while I put down the phone. In the hopes of finding Gofer a home, I was willing to try almost anything. Sarah and I went to find Gofer, who was off playing with several of my new rescues. We were giggling once again because neither of us wanted to be knocked over by Gofer, who was already sort of a bumbling buffoon. Knowing him, he would jump up and land on both of our heads.

I told Sarah the name we were supposed to use, and I was elected to try it first since I had more muscle on my body from lifting weights. I could more easily withstand a beating from our hyperactive but incredibly sweet oaf.

I caught Gofer's attention, stretched out my arms in front of me and said, "Putty, up!"

In an instant, his body elevated and landed directly into my arms. I was a bit stunned so I thought I would have Sarah try it. She stretched out her arms while giggling and said, "Putty, up!" The same thing happened.

While we were both laughing, I looked at Gofer, who was staring at me, panting, and asked, "Is your name Putty?"

He cocked his head and began spinning, barking at us and circling with joy, as if he had just regained his identity. Sarah and I couldn't believe it, and kept taking turns having our oaf jump into our arms on command. With both of our mouths wide open in disbelief, Sarah said, in all of her brilliance, "No way, Randi. You know what? Gofer isn't the wild, unsocialized, untrained dog we thought he was at our adoptions. He was jumping out of the puppy pen and landing on people to greet them because his dad had trained him to do that. I guess the vet just misjudged his age. They do that all of the time."

Sarah and I returned to the phone to find Steven patiently waiting on the other end. I caught my breath from all of the excitement and

Steven and Gofer hugging after
their long separation

said, "When can you come to Encino? We have your dog. Your search is over."

Sarah and I clearly understood the divine reason why Gofer was never adopted from our rescue. We reunited Gofer—now Putty—with his father the following day. When Putty jumped into his dad's arms, the tears of joy were shared by all of us. Sitting on our kitchen floor, they embraced with an intensity that we had never before seen.

In one magnificent twenty-four-hour period, five dogs and their humans were brought together in the most miraculous ways. It was, without a doubt, a day Saint Francis of Assisi, patron saint of animals, was watching over us with a smile.

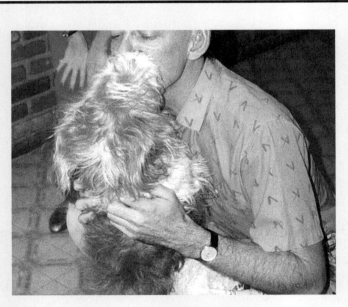

Steven and Gofer/Putty kissing after being reunited

CHAPTER 9

A LITTLE BLACK MAGIC
IN MY LIFE
September 22, 1993

God, how I miss you. It's only been hours since you left, but my insides are aching for you.

It was Friday, August 13, and as usual I had more dogs for adoption than I had expected. But I was driving past an animal shelter in Southern California and "had" to stop and look. I told myself I could take only a small young female dog, because I knew I could place one like that quickly.

Adoptions this summer had started out better than any in my six years of rescuing. Usually, summers are very slow with an abundance of owners giving up their dogs and few adoptions. But several weeks before this, my adoptions had come to a halt, and I was again getting more returns and owner give-up dogs than people wanting to adopt dogs.

As I cruised by the packed runs of this shelter, I was ready to leave when I saw that the only available dog who appeared semi-adoptable was a black male Poodle mix mounting everything, including the air! I didn't need this in my life right now. The veterinary technician, Janet, came up to me, hoping I would take the above-mentioned dog, when I noticed something hiding under a feeder bin in the same run. It was definitely a male and definitely black, the most difficult combination to place. But I was curious since it didn't move and appeared too frightened even to lie down. He was just sitting there, staring at the ground and hiding. We pulled his card from his cage, which said, "owner turn-in 'Magic'" and in big red letters, written by a kennel worker, "CAUTION!"

Janet was one of the more cooperative veterinary technicians I knew and went into this dog's cage to look at him for me. She attempted to pick up Magic, but he whipped his head around as though he was going to bite. She took her pen to gently lift his lip to look at his teeth so that we could determine his age, but again he went to snap at her. He looked so alone and invaded, as if the only person he wanted touching him was the person for whom he was so obviously grieving. His coat was healthy and beautifully groomed. Someone had loved and cared for this dog. I wished we knew what had happened, and I wished there was a way to let Magic's previous owner know that, with Magic's fear of strangers, this shelter could not keep him for adoption. As an owner turn-in, he was immediately considered abandoned and unwanted and was now on the list to be put to sleep.

The first time I had met Janet, she seemed quite cold and angry. It didn't take long for me to see a smile crack on her face, and I then realized that her aloofness was merely a façade. As long as you weren't one of the many people abandoning an animal at her overcrowded shelter, she was as helpful, open, and caring as Mother Teresa.

Janet worked at one of the worst shelters in Southern California, where the majority of the animals that came in were severely neglected or abused. Backyard breeding, professional dog-fighting, and cock-fighting rings were very common in the large area served by this shelter. The look of disgust that Janet gave to many of the people walking through her shelter was more than justified. But once Janet knew you were a mildly sane animal rescuer, her face would soften and she would welcome your arrival.

Janet didn't think twice about breaking the rules at her shelter to help save a dog's life and brought Magic out to the fenced play area so we could attempt to handle him, hopefully breaking through his protective shell. He was still very distant, but as we called his name, he would come toward us and then sit with his back to us. He did not want to be touched though and continued whipping his head around as if he were going to bite when we approached him. As I saw the abandonment in his eyes, mine began to tear, and I knew I could not let this little "Magic" be destroyed. It seemed that he wanted to trust, but the risk was too great at this time in his life.

Although Janet would be the one euthanizing the unwanted dogs, including Magic, at the end of the day, she said, "Randi, are you sure about this one? I would love to see him get out of here, but I think he may be a problem. He's been here five days and hasn't warmed up to any of us."

"Oh, Janet, I don't know. He's the last thing I need in my life right now, but I sense there's something special about him. He seems more sensitive than most, and maybe being abandoned and stuck in this loud, crowded place has traumatized him."

This was a big dilemma for me as Magic was definitely not a small, young, adoptable female. It was also Friday the thirteenth, and in the back of my mind, I had to wonder if I was making a big mistake. Would this be a rescue dog who would bite me or seriously injure others? I thought it might be a curse, but I couldn't walk away from him with peace of mind. He reminded me of Goose and had the same look of fear on his face. I just couldn't leave him there.

Janet smiled at me as she signed off his kennel card, releasing him to me.

So on Friday, August 13, I made a commitment to Magic, not knowing what would be in store as I never was able to touch him.

Janet sent him out to be neutered the next day, and I was to pick him up from a local twenty-four-hour vet that following evening. I phoned the vet in the morning to alert the staff: "A dog is coming in from the shelter to be neutered. I bailed him out of there yesterday. He's very scared, and I was wondering if you could flush out his ears while he's still under the anesthesia. I was unable to handle him and it looks as if one of his ears may be infected. I don't think he'll let me treat him when he is awake."

"Are you talking about Magic?" the veterinary receptionist asked. "That dog is so nasty the vet wants him out of here as soon as possible. We were barely able to handle him for his neuter. We took care of him first thing in the morning so that he could go home early. He's awake and ready to go now. How soon can you pick him up?"

"Is there any way he can be sedated again so that his ears can be cleaned out and medicated?" I asked. "I was hoping to pick him up while he was still groggy. I'm holding an open house adoption this weekend, and I wanted to give him a bath before then. I don't think he'll let me do anything to him if he's fully awake. I don't mind paying for it."

"Let me ask the vet," the receptionist said, while she put me on hold.

She returned and said, "The vet wants him out of here. We're very crowded and this dog is too difficult to handle. Again, how soon can you get here?"

I had planned to pick up Magic at the end of the day but rearranged my schedule to immediately get him out of this clinic where he was apparently so loathed. The thought of him being in the company of anyone lacking the patience to understand what he must be going through saddened me.

When I arrived at the veterinary clinic, the receptionist asked me to get him out of the cage so as to keep any of the staff from being bitten. Magic must have still been sedated from the anesthesia because he let me pick him up and sat in my lap, completely still, on the way home. So far, everything was going better than expected.

Magic let me carry him into my house, and when I took him out to the grass in the backyard, he immediately went to the bathroom as if on command. This was almost too easy to be true. I wondered if the vet who had just neutered him may have slipped him a strong dose of Prozac or some other mood-enhancing drug. Perhaps it was just the residual sedative effect from the anesthesia.

I was able to put Magic in the tub with no problem, but was now a bit fearful, realizing that he was absolutely no longer at all sedated. It figured. Most dogs are pretty drowsy from the anesthesia until the next morning. But the one I was worried about handling was the only one I had ever known who was wide awake immediately after surgery.

I soon discovered that it didn't matter. As I was bathing Magic, he began to stare at me and within minutes gave me my first kiss on his own. Oh God, I was falling in love again! He ended up being one of the easiest dogs I've ever groomed and even let me cut his toenails while giving me periodic kisses. I realized that to divert his attention from his fear, all I needed to do was kiss him and he'd kiss me back.

Magic was very scared and confused at the adoptions the next day. I brought him home, integrating him instantly with my own dogs. I wanted to be with him and comfort him through this rough time in his life. He was very shy and withdrawn and truly seemed to be grieving the loss of his "person."

Magic was more sensitive than the others, and his spirits didn't change throughout that week. He did begin to attach himself to me, and I to him, as I now had a mission to see his tail wag. He was always very gentle, polite, and quiet, as though he didn't want to impose himself on us. My own "kids" treated him as if he had always been there and returned his gentleness.

The week had passed with Magic slowly coming out of his depression. I awoke on a Saturday and realized that Magic was not able to move. When I gently petted his head, he screamed and was not able to stand up. Why him? I rushed him to my emergency vet, where he was given an injection for the pain. We never were quite clear with what was wrong. By my Sunday adoptions he was fine, but I was getting even more attached, watching him suffer through another trauma.

Magic showed much better at my adoptions the next day although he never took his eyes off of me. A mother came in with her eight-year-old son who kept turning his attention to Magic. The boy said to his mom, "This one is my favorite. Can we get him?"

I was hoping the adoption application that the mother filled out would be awful. I instantly rejected applications that indicated plans for or a history of keeping a dog outside, giving away a pet in the past, returning a dog for behavioral problems, and the like. Because we often have multiple people wanting to adopt the same dog, we are afforded the luxury of being able to be extremely discerning with the people we select. Unfortunately, these people who were interested in Magic were as perfect as any rescue could hope for as new dog parents, and Magic was their choice. I was hoping to be stuck with him a little longer, but no such luck. He never snapped or hid from this little boy and actually was quite affectionate with him.

One of my volunteers went to their house to make sure all was okay, and it was so busy at my adoptions that day that it truly didn't sink in until the middle of the night when I awoke to Magic's absence. My heart dropped. I wanted him back.

My wish came true. Two days later, the mom phoned and said, "Randi, I'm so heartbroken, and we feel so bad. My youngest daughter is allergic to Magic. I don't think we can have any pets at all. He is the most wonderful, well-behaved little gentleman. There's no dog I've ever met like him. He is an absolute treasure. But it does seem that he is grieving and may be a little depressed."

I didn't think it would be appropriate to let too much of my excitement come through in my voice so I tried to contain myself and calmly said, "Oh, I'm so sorry. I can come right now and get him," even though I was swamped with work and calls that needed to be returned.

As I drove up to their house and was reunited with my newest love, it was apparent that I was the one for whom Magic had been grieving this time. He ran up to me and jumped up on me to hold him. I knew then that he would probably become a permanent love in my life. I couldn't place him again. He was too sensitive to go through that and be traumatized one more time.

This was a rough period in my life. Adoptions were now at a standstill, and I was getting very sick and overwhelmed. I would look at my new little man and say, "I need some Magic in my life," and he'd pop up into my arms and cuddle against my face. Magic and I were becoming inseparable. When I had him at my adoptions, he'd never leave my side. He'd follow my every move, never losing sight of where I was. The name Magic seemed to have some sad connotation for him, so his new, happier name became Pooh Bear.

In the next week, Pooh Bear, in addition to the ear infection for which I was treating him, contracted a severe case of diarrhea. The week after that, I awoke one morning to find his eyes crusted shut. As I went to look at them, he screamed out of pain. Off again to the vet, where we discovered he had a severe eye infection that might take his sight. As Pooh Bear was becoming less adoptable, I was becoming more attached to him, which I typically don't allow myself to do.

As a bit more time passed, I hesitated in telling prospective adopters about Pooh Bear, who was now also given another nickname—Muffin. Once in a rare while, I would show dogs at my house if I felt comfortable with the people. Such a couple came to me, looking at a scruffy little eight-pound terrier mix. They had had a miniature schnauzer named Muffin, who had passed away, and a depressed golden retriever in need of a new sibling.

When Lynn and Jerry were sitting in my kitchen looking at this terrier mix, Googles, a.k.a. Sewer Rat, I mentioned that I also had a Muffin, who had recently become too near and dear to my heart for me to place.

"Could we meet him?" Lynn asked.

"I would love to bring him out," I said, "but he's often snappy with strangers and will do nothing but hide under a chair and bark at you."

"Please let us just take a quick peek at him," they said simultaneously. They reminded me of young children begging their parents to stay up late, and I couldn't resist their innocence.

I again warned them, "You won't be able to touch him, but you can at least see what I've most recently become attached to out of the hundreds of dogs a year who cross my path. I'll be right back."

As I was walking away, Lynn said, "I've never met a dog who didn't instantly fall in love with my husband."

This couple truly was amazing. Jerry was an exceptionally tall man with an incredible gentleness about him. Lynn glowed with a peacefulness that I somewhat envied at this time in my hectic, overwhelming life. It seemed apparent that these two very much honored their marriage vows as they still, after years of being together, looked at each other with the eyes of newlyweds. They both raved about each other to me, almost as though they were trying to sell me on each other as superior dog parents. But I was sold after talking to them on the phone, even before meeting them. Now, after seeing them in person, I wanted their peaceful, calm, and positive energy never to leave my house.

Lynn and Jerry's lives existed for their dogs. They never left their dogs alone and never went on vacation. Jerry built handicap ramps throughout their house for their dogs, who were their only children. But most impressive to me was the fact that neither of these two beautiful people ever stopped smiling. If they did adopt one of my dogs, I was considering adding a clause to the contract stating that they also agreed to adopt me!

I left the kitchen to do a quick dog swap and returned with Magic/Pooh Bear/Muffin, who completely ignored Lynn and Jerry's gentle

Googles, a.k.a. Sewer Rat
with new friends

Lynn and our
little black Magic

energy. As expected, he hid under my chair and then incessantly started barking at them with a look on his face that said, "This is it. They're both here to end my life. They came here to kill me." The only time he stopped barking at them was when they looked away from him. This went on for about ten minutes when I finally just picked up Muffin and handed him to Jerry, who couldn't wait to hold him. Although this was the first dog that they had ever met who didn't instantly gravitate to their safe, saint-like energy, both Lynn and Jerry were intrigued by him. When they ignored him and he stopped barking, he would back up to Jerry and sit by him. Neither of them feared being bitten by Muffin.

After only a couple of minutes in big Jerry's arms, Muffin began kissing his face. Jerry held Muffin up to Lynn's face, and she was also given a bath by Muffin's tongue. After about fifteen minutes of this, Jerry put Muffin down on the ground, and the incessant barking instantly returned.

Muffin had one of the most unusual temperaments I'd ever seen, and I adored every quirk in his little body and mind. After over an hour with Muffin, Lynn and Jerry felt they had kept me too long and said they would stay in touch. I really wouldn't have minded if they had never left, as my house and I enjoyed their energy.

When several days passed and I hadn't heard from Lynn and Jerry, I assumed that they had decided to wait for another dog. But the next day, Lynn left a message on my voice mail saying that she needed to talk to me. When I returned her call, she could barely form her words as she slowly said, "Randi, there were too many coincidences with Muffin. As you know, our dog who passed away was named Muffin. But I didn't tell you when we were at your house that he was also nicknamed Pooh Bear. Who would have believed us? There are some other things I want to tell you. We really would like to meet Muffin again and see if he would let us adopt him."

I couldn't imagine holding onto Muffin now. It would have only been selfish to do so. As much as I knew it would hurt to let him go, nothing in Muffin's life could have ever been better for him than ending up with Lynn and Jerry.

I spent the next two days emotionally preparing to say good-bye to Muffin and to gracefully follow through with his adoption. On the day we decided to meet, I waited outside of my house, holding Muffin in my arms and hoping he wouldn't again greet Lynn and Jerry with his incessant barking. In my mind, this adoption had now already happened.

This glowing couple walked up to us, smiling, and Muffin did seem to forget who they were. He carried on with his fearful barking, and Jerry simply took him into his arms, coddling him like a baby. They walked Muffin around my neighborhood for a while, giving him some time to bond with them before taking him away from me.

I went into my house and anxiously kept looking out the window, spying on them, hoping Muffin could trust them without me by his side. About fifteen minutes later, Lynn and Jerry came back with Muffin in their arms, giving both of them an abundance of kisses. Once again, I didn't want this to end and have this new family leave.

After we completed all of the paperwork and Lynn and Jerry were hugging me good-bye, Lynn told me of a dream she had had weeks earlier, before ever speaking to me.

"Randi, I just couldn't tell you this over the phone. After our other Muffin had died, I had a dream about a little black dog. This dog came running up to me in my dream. His name was Magic."

As the tears welled up in all of our eyes, it now became very clear to me as to why Magic's life needed to be spared.

CHAPTER 10

THE LOVE OF A LHASA
January 17, 1994

I t felt like the end of the world, as if the earth had spun off its axis. My own dogs, who usually barked at any intrusive noise or movement, were completely still and quiet. Outside it was eerie, quiet, and dark for miles. It seemed as if we'd never see daylight again. I was grabbing heads, as many as I could feel in the darkness, to protect my dogs from falling objects or the true possibility of the house collapsing in on us.

It was January 17, 1994, and the Great Northridge earthquake had just hit. My love for a new breed would develop as a result of one of the heads that emerged from under my arm when the shaking finally stopped.

Khan was a five-year-old Lhasa apso who came to me in the autumn of 1993. A pickup truck pulled up in front of Martex Pet Shop in Encino, where I was holding my adoptions that Saturday afternoon. An unassuming older gentleman slowly approached me and patiently waited in line to talk to me. He quietly stood with his hands tucked into the back pockets of his blue jeans for about twenty minutes before the crowd of people cleared and he could get to me.

"Hi, are you Randi?" he asked. I reached out to shake his hand. "Khan's dad?" I replied. "I'm sorry you had to wait so long."

Khan's dad was a gentle sort of man, not the type who seemed likely to be giving up a pet. As he was talking to me, the only thing I could focus on was the face staring at us out of the passenger window of his truck. It resembled a stuffed toy that had come to life after falling off a shelf in a children's shop.

I pointed to the face that looked too irresistibly cute to be real and asked, "Is that Khan?"

The detached older man nodded. "Yes, it is. Do you think you can take him today?"

"How can you part with that face?" I asked. "His cheeks look like big, fat, peach muffins. I've never seen anything like him in my life. Does he move at all?"

Khan's father smiled while responding in a monotone voice, "He is a very calm boy. He's the best, easiest pet I've ever had, but my grand-children are moving in with me, and it's going to be too much to have him around. I wish I could keep him. I brought some of his things with me in case you could take him today."

"I think I have room," I said. "But are you sure you're ready to let him go?"

"I'd just as soon do it today," he said as he walked over to his truck. He opened the passenger door to let out "the stuffed toy."

When Khan saw his dad pick up his leash, he came to life, bouncing up and down and acting as though they had just been reunited after a ten-year separation.

When I saw Khan's big sad eyes watch his father drive away, leaving him behind, I realized that he reminded me of Bambi. That entire day at my adoptions, Khan sat completely still and never stopped staring in the direction he had watched his father leave. It seemed as if he was waiting for his father to come back for him.

Khan was one of the dogs I brought home with me that evening since he wasn't adopted. His demeanor was quite reticent, and he crept through our house so quietly that it seemed as if he was walking in plush slippers.

My mom was never quite sure which faces were new, as the hundreds of dogs that infiltrated her house over the years seemed now to be blending together in her mind. Several days after Khan had been with us, he appeared at her feet when she was sitting at her makeup table, preparing to meet with clients. Khan just sat there quietly, staring up at her for about five minutes, when she finally looked down at him. I was sitting on her bed with a smirk on my face, watching the two of them, while anticipating her reaction. I couldn't wait to see if she would notice that Khan was a new dog. When she realized that his peach, pumpkin-shaped face was one that she hadn't before seen, she commented in disbelief, "Oh my God! That's the cutest dog you've ever brought in this house! We need to keep this one!"

Whew! I breathed a sigh of relief. Khan and I were safe.

I would often go unconscious, bringing more dogs into Mom's house than any sane dog-loving person would want. My mom either begged me to keep most of them, as she became attached upon first glimpse of any homeless animal, or wanted to divorce me. While it seemed as though I was born with the keen ability to easily detach, which enabled me to love and let go, my mom wanted to hold on to *everything* that crossed her path. She even fell in love with the cardboard inserts from toilet paper rolls and kept drawers full of them. No one ever knew why, but she had her "logical" reasons that the lawyer in her was able to justify.

The upside to this was that she was the best dog foster mom in the world. But she would occasionally play the victim role, saying, "Randi, I never asked for any of these dogs! Stop bringing them here!" The truth was that most of them ended up sleeping in her bed and watching TV with her. She went into debt replacing a window in her bedroom with a Dutch door to our backyard. Then she had a covered patio built off it so no dogs would ever float away in the rain when they would go outside to relieve themselves. Now, keep in mind, it only rains about two weeks a year in Southern California, if we're lucky. Then she connected a ramp to her bed so that our many elderly and short-legged dogs would not be humiliated by having to ask for a boost to get on and off her bed. No one had the courage to suggest that she go for help when she began working from home, believing that no dog should ever be without a human. This was when she moved a long table next to her bed so that all of her dogs could sit right with her when she was working. Then she draped blankets all around that table to form a tent, where one of our agoraphobic dogs, Ernest, was more than content residing like a king. Her bedroom became overstuffed with "necessary" canine accouterments, and there was barely any room for a human to walk through it.

Our role reversal kicked in at this time, and I began setting the rules, often saying, "No, Marcie, you cannot keep this one. It's entirely adoptable."

She would respond, "Then stop bringing them in my house. I get too attached."

These little spats continued until I finally faced her one day and said, "Marcie, do you really want me to take all of the dogs out of here? I will take all of them to other foster homes if you honestly don't want them here."

She paused for a moment and then surrendered, saying in a childlike voice, "I would die without them."

The one thing that my mom and I absolutely agreed on was that Khan was one of the most scrumptious-looking dogs we had ever seen. However, he had one insurmountable problem—he lacked any personality. He was indifferent with humans and dogs. I couldn't have agreed more with his father; Khan was a very easy dog to have in the house, so much so he seemed like a robot. He ate when I fed him, immediately went to the bathroom when I took him out, never barked, and never asked for any attention.

After having him with me for several weeks, I realized that something must be wrong. Most of the time, I had kept Khan with the other adoption dogs, separate from my own, and was so busy that I didn't realize how depressed he must have been. Happy dogs didn't act like this. All of the other adoption dogs seemed to adjust quickly after coming to me. They would play, bark, and ask for love. I was soon to learn about winning over the love of a Lhasa.

This breed wasn't one I had often rescued. They seemed too perfect to me, too desirable. I preferred the scruffy, insecure mixes that I felt needed me. When I realized how sad Khan still was after weeks of being without his owner, I began to integrate him with my own dogs to see if he would respond to my affection. Now I discovered why Khan was truly given away.

This dog didn't seem to like being touched much. He would growl and snap at you if you left your hand on him for more than three seconds. One day my mom and I timed it. So she figured out a way that she could love him without using her hands. If she put her head down on the bed, Khan would come up to her and press his round, puffy head against hers, grunting against her face and snuggling up for a minute or two. This appeared to be rapturous for both of them—as long as she didn't touch him with her hands.

Khan barely tolerated being held, and it seemed I was the only one who understood how to pick him up without being bitten. Another thing that I learned about Khan was that you didn't go near anything of "his." Other than that, he was a perfect dog.

All of these traits emerged, as he became more comfortable with my mom, his new home, and me. I began to think I actually preferred the depressed Khan. The more I got to know him, the less adoptable he became. But nothing about him was unpredictable. We knew when he was going to bite. I knew not to take tissues and earplugs out of his mouth. In one of our battles of the will when I needed to get mail out of his mouth that he thought belonged to him, he was staring at me with his big Bambi eyes, and I just began to laugh. He always seemed to win because his big, fat, peach muffin face and sad Bambi eyes made me give into him. This was when I began calling him Bam Bam, and realized that this breed was one of the most headstrong, difficult breeds I had ever known.

Although people admired Bam Bam's looks when I had him at my adoptions, he didn't want anyone touching him or walking him. When I would put a leash on him for people to walk him, he would flatten himself out on the ground and put on his brakes. Rigor mortis would set into his body if I handed him to anyone who was willing to overlook his foibles. One man walked away from my adoptions after failing to find even the slightest redeeming personality trait in Bam Bam, and I heard him say to his wife, "Why don't they change his name to Grumpy?"

Bam Bam didn't seem to like me more than anyone else after being with me for more than two months. Unfortunately, he was beginning to feel like my dog. He still never showed any affection toward me and only tolerated me. Although he did sleep in bed with me, he still didn't

Bam Bam and adoptee, Sparkleberry, expressing Lhasa love

want to be touched. I had never met such an aloof dog in my life. I couldn't understand why anyone would want a Lhasa.

On this particular night, I went to sleep at around 3 a.m., my normal time. I was awakened shortly after by the most devastating disaster in the history of Los Angeles, the Northridge earthquake. I could hear buildings crumbling and glass breaking around me. It seemed as if the shaking would never stop. I was grateful that my dogs were all near me. When the shaking stopped and the sun finally rose, which seemed like a lifetime, I was more shocked about Bam Bam's head being under one of my arms than I was about the earthquake itself. This was the first and only time he came to me and wanted to be touched. It almost seemed as if Bam Bam was embarrassed to admit that after a 6.9 earthquake, he needed me.

My own dogs fared well, at least physically. Our house had minimal damage with only broken glass and objects strewn everywhere. The news advised us not to leave our homes for many days because of the collapsed buildings and horrendous aftershocks.

I had almost entirely stopped rescuing dogs from shelters because of the many owner-give-up calls I had been receiving. I was now taking dogs from their owners to prevent them from ending up in the shelters. But after this earthquake, I began receiving many calls from traumatized people who had lost their dogs, either by walls collapsing and the dogs running off in fear or by objects falling on them and killing them. The only thing I wanted to do now was get to the local shelters to help the hundreds of lost and injured dogs.

On my first trip out of the house, a week after the earthquake, I was shocked by how many dogs and cats I saw running on the streets and lying on the sides of the road dead. My destination was the animal shelter in Northridge, the epicenter of the earthquake. It was only ten minutes from where I live. I hadn't cried walking through a shelter in years. I had become immune to the pain after seeing it several times a week. But seeing this shelter was an entire disaster in itself. The dog runs were jammed with frightened eyes and shaking bodies. Many of the dogs' paws were cut from the broken glass and debris. A new illness had developed, called Valley Fever, a fungal infection that begins in the lungs. It affects people and animals alike, and some animals were already dying from it. Due to overcrowding, this shelter now had to begin placing the animals that the workers had been trying to hold for their owners. I began taking out as many dogs as possible in hopes of reuniting them with their parents. But many people lost their homes in this tragedy and were unable to take back their pets. Seeing how the most macho of men crumbled emotionally from this broke my own heart. I wondered what the most frail and innocent unknowing animals must have felt.

I attempted to carry on my weekend adoptions at Martex Pet Shop, but very few people who lived in Southern California were in the mood to adopt a pet. Bam Bam continued to come with me to my adoptions. We were having monumental aftershocks from the quake and one was so big that we saw a huge window blast out of its frames across the street in an office building next to Fromin's Deli, an Encino landmark.

Bam Bam was having a difficult time maintaining his stoic personality through these aftershocks. As the aftershocks increased in magnitude, Bam Bam's ability to maintain his standoffish nature decreased. He was at his wits' end when the biggest aftershock came. He put his oversized, plush slipper paws up on me to hold him, with his Bambi eyes melting my heart. I was the only person whose existence Bam Bam acknowledged in almost three months. It seemed pointless to continue bringing him to the adoptions as he ignored anyone who was interested in him. He had no desire to sell himself the way the other dogs did.

I actually began to admire Bam Bam's discriminating nature as I realized that his breed is like no other. Over the months, he finally bonded with me, but remained the most irresistibly aloof dog I have ever loved.

Because of Bam Bam, I began helping many Lhasa apsos. I now understand that there is more to them than just their good looks. This is not a breed for everyone. Those who are thin-skinned, needy, or insecure should look elsewhere. But anyone who has figured out how to win the love of a Lhasa would never replace it with any other breed. Because of Bam Bam, I couldn't comprehend life without a Lhasa.

CHAPTER 11

STARR'S STORY
April 27, 1996

With my preference to help the older or abused dogs, it was unusual to hear the pitter-patter of puppies' paws in my house. But four times along my rescuing path, I made an exception and acquired mothers with puppies or very pregnant females who were ready to burst with them. Starr was an unborn puppy with a memorable story. Most of my focus always seemed to go to the dogs. But this adoption would be an exception.

Michelle was heartbroken about the recent loss of her dog, Tia Maria, and went on like a chatterbox when we first spoke on the phone. There was no possible way I could let every person who called go on and on about past beloved pets. There simply was not enough time in the day to hear everyone's stories, and I would often feel frustrated as I was unable to escape many people's impassioned vignettes recounting their dog's entire life. Michelle was no exception other than the fact that it seemed that she had either ingested far too much caffeine or had an unparalleled zest for life, despite her sadness about her late Lhasa apso mix love. But Michelle was different from the rest and engaged me with her enthusiasm and voice, which resembled those of a six-year-old. I was unsure about Michelle's age, but as she opened up, immediately telling me more than I wanted to know, I realized that she was definitely not a child.

"So, anyway, when I'm at my apartment in Japan, running my music production company, Sweetheart Productions, my mom, Dorothy, would be here with our new baby. Oh my God, Randi, we didn't know how we would survive losing her. It was devastating to us. She was our angel, and we feel so lost without her. We'll wait as long as it takes to find our new baby. We really need another little girl who is a fluff-ball, romantic kisser. We don't want to go to a breeder. We really want to rescue a dog."

"Do you live with your mom when you're out here in the States?" I asked.

"Oh, yes! We're best friends! She's a paralegal, but her life would revolve around our new little girl the way it did with Tia Maria," Michelle exuberantly replied. "Do you want to talk to my mom? She's standing right over me listening to our entire conversation. She's been adding little comments, reminding me to tell you about certain things."

Again it was difficult to tell just how old Michelle was, and I didn't want to be so rude as to ask. But I was curious because I thought I was one of the only mildly functional adult females still living with my mother and proudly admitting it.

I never had to ask Michelle one question about herself since she continued to divulge her entire life to me in our first conversation. It didn't take long to discover that our lives and our unusual closeness to our mothers were strangely similar. I felt blessed to have the honor of filling the void in their lives.

"Michelle," I said, "I think I may already have your new little girl."

"Oh my God, Randi! We would be so grateful to you. When can we come and see her?" Michelle asked.

I could hear Dorothy in the background saying, "Tell her we can come tomorrow."

"Is tomorrow morning okay?" Michelle asked.

"I'm sorry," I said. "That won't be possible."

Michelle respectfully apologized. "Oh, I'm sure you must be so busy. I'm sorry. We're so ready to bring a new little girl into our lives that we're both very eager. We can come whenever you're available."

"That has nothing to do with it," I said. "The problem is that the dog has yet to be born. I recently rescued a very pregnant Maltese from a woman who was ready to take her to the shelter. She had to give up her dog, Crystal, due to financial hardship. She was never even able to afford to spay her and believed that Crystal's play dates with a neighbor's poodle led to her becoming pregnant. When the woman phoned the animal shelter to turn in her dog, ready to burst with puppies, the shelter gave her my phone number. They would have immediately put Crystal to sleep in her condition."

"Do you know if there may be a girl in the litter?" Michelle asked.

"I have no idea, and I don't even know when they will be born. I'm a novice at this puppy thing, but I promise to call you guys the day they are born. It could even be today. I hope your new baby girl will be one of them," I said.

"Oh my God, Randi! We're so excited! Would we be bothering you if we continue to check back with you?"

"No! You feel like you could be my sister. I've never spoken to anyone who seems so much like myself. I hope to call you with the news very soon. And Michelle," I said, "if this doesn't work out, I promise to help you find your new little girl."

I only had one previous experience with newborn puppies, so my nervousness seemed to parallel Michelle's. We spoke often, waiting to see what would be born from Crystal's tiny body.

When that day soon came, it turned out that Michelle was working in Japan. I relayed the information to her mother, Dorothy.

"Hi, it's Randi! The first one was a little girl followed by two boys. They are all apricot in color, but the girl has a teeny white mark on her head and it seems to resemble a star. I don't usually name puppies because they would never get to know their names before they were quickly adopted. But this little girl is a character and prances around like a little shining ballerina. I've never seen a puppy like her and have already started calling her Starr."

As exuberant as Michelle was, I found Dorothy to be the opposite. She calmly said, "Very good then. Thank you for calling, Randi. I'm not sure when Michelle will be back, but I'll let her know right away. I assume we won't be able to see them for awhile since they were just born. Do you mind us keeping in touch with you?"

One thing that was identical about Michelle and Dorothy was their incredible respect and politeness, which I so appreciated. Many of the voices on the other end of my phone were demanding and occasionally rude when it came to the rescue. Some people acted as though they believed that the volunteers who helped run animal rescue organizations were high-paid employees who should be at their beck and call. But many of us are unpaid, full-time volunteers, scrambling to stay afloat financially. Some have accumulated astronomical debts that have resulted from the never-ending need to help unwanted animals. But I've always maintained my faith that the means to support this "habit" would continue to reveal itself in one form or another.

So, dealing with Michelle and Dorothy was a complete pleasure. No matter how often they phoned, I welcomed both of their voices. It turned out that over thirty people wanted Crystal and her three puppies, but I knew where Starr belonged.

I was quite protective and wouldn't let them be seen by anyone until they were approximately six weeks old, waiting another few weeks for them to go to their new homes. I had invited those thirty people to the puppies' first showing at a pet shop in Tarzana called Pet-Xtra. It was a madhouse, with everyone falling over each other to see Starr, her two brothers and their mom. Michelle and Dorothy were the only people who remained calm and collected, standing back and watching from a distance. Everyone else was pushing in to hold Crystal, her two kissing, bouncing sons and Starr, who was off on her own with no interest in participating in any of this.

Michelle and Dorothy now seemed hesitant, as though maybe Starr wasn't the one for them. Their ambivalence caused me sadly now to have second thoughts about placing Starr with them.

Michelle had a major problem. The only two prerequisites for the dog with whom she was hoping to spend the next fifteen or so years were that it be a girl and that that girl be a big "kisser." The two brothers were jumping up to kiss everyone, but Starr was not. Starr was acting like a snooty princess, who would not give herself freely to just anyone. Michelle was in such a dilemma that she even had her brother, Jason, who was visiting from New York, come to meet Starr. Jason immediately fell in love with Starr and thought she was very bright. He convinced Michelle that Starr would warm up and most likely become "a kisser" like her brothers.

I overheard Michelle say, "But Jason, I don't care about bright or smart. I need romantic and kissy. She won't even kiss me at all, and she seems extremely boring to me."

This wasn't a decision to be made lightly for Michelle and Dorothy, but the more time they spent with Starr, the more she began to feel like theirs—except for the fact that no matter what Michelle did, she could not get Starr to kiss her. I didn't mind accommodating them, and I let them visit Starr in my home several times before the big adoption day. I really didn't feel anyone but Michelle and Dorothy was worthy of adopting Starr, but I didn't want to push them into something that did not feel right for both of them. For Michelle and Dorothy, this was a "forever" decision.

Adoption day finally came for the three puppies and their mom, with mild postpartum depression for me. Needless to say, Starr went home with Michelle and Dorothy, with Michelle ranting and raving about Starr's unwillingness to kiss.

The surprise came for me when I received one of my many calls from Michelle and Dorothy later that day. Both of them were exuberantly talking at the same time and then Michelle said, "Guess what, Auntie Randi. I wasn't going to kiss anyone until they made a commitment to me. Why should I give all of myself before they would?" Michelle added, "Starr wanted us to tell you that the second we got her home, she began kissing us."

Then Dorothy jumped in: "I can't believe this little girl, Randi. It was like a game for her. She hasn't stopped kissing us from the moment we made the commitment and held her in our laps on the way home."

Months later, in one of my many chats with Michelle, she said, "Oh my God. I can't believe it, Randi! The older Starr gets, the more she looks just like Tia Maria. In photographs you can't even tell the two apart. You changed our lives!"

It was in that same conversation, months after Starr had been with Michelle and Dorothy, when Michelle asked me for the actual date Starr was born.

I said, "Hold on one minute. I have to go through my paper work. I'll be right back." I thought I had given them that information, but apparently I hadn't.

When I returned and gave Michelle Starr's birth date, April 27, she became silent for the first time since I had known her. Michelle and Starr shared the same birthday.

The prima donna, Starr!

CHAPTER 12

HEIDI'S STORY
Spring 1996

For a long time, I couldn't understand the appeal of dachshunds. They looked to me like something one would call the exterminator to have removed from his garage. What could be so enticing about cuddling up with an oversized, bald rodent? I was soon to be in for the surprise of my life!

I received an owner-give-up call about two dachshunds. I hadn't before rescued certain breeds with which I was unfamiliar or to which I was not attracted, just in case I ended up not being able to place that dog. My permanent, four-legged family is comprised of these "unadoptables," and the thought of a dachshund fitting into this menagerie was less than appealing.

When Heidi and Pepper's mother phoned me, I tried to send her to Dachshund Rescue, but she name-dropped in the only way that would ever impress me and said, "The Trockers in Calabasas highly recommended you. We were neighbors of theirs but had significant damage to our house from the Northridge earthquake." This woman knew what to say to get my attention. The Trockers were one of my favorite families, who adopted their first puppies, Mindy and Cody, from me. They were so very endearing as nervous, new dog parents, and we stayed in contact while I educated them on the agonies and ecstasies of puppyhood.

The woman continued, "We have mother and daughter dachshunds and can no longer keep them. The reconstruction of our house is taking longer than expected, and we have no idea when it will be finished. The mother, Heidi, is fourteen and her daughter, Pepper, is only nine. They've always been together, and I think they should stay together."

I was hoping that she meant fourteen and nine months, but I realized that would have been physically impossible. This woman clearly had no concept of what was considered adoptable in the world of dog rescue. Nine years old was far past the age that almost anyone would adopt. Fourteen was beyond the life-span of many dogs. But this woman continued to remind me how much the Trockers bragged about their dogs and appreciated the help that I gave them through the adoption process.

I patiently let her continue speaking. "Heidi and Pepper are very sweet, and they share a basket that they sleep in together outside. They just love that. They put themselves to sleep in it and burrow under the blankets, disappearing until the morning."

This is when I finally asked, "Have they been outside dogs?" The main reason people adopt adult dogs is because they don't want to go through the puppy training and housebreaking. I couldn't envision anyone lining up to adopt a pair of fourteen- and nine-year-old untrained dogs.

"Oh, they love it outside. We tried keeping them inside, but they went to the bathroom everywhere. Heidi is almost completely blind, so you have to be careful when you approach her or she'll bite you. They love their squeaky toys too!"

Great! I thought to myself. Could she say anything more that could make these dogs any less adoptable? But she continued on, boasting about Heidi and Pepper as if she believed many people would covet having them in their lives.

I finally stopped her and said, "I have to be honest with you. Most people won't adopt dogs over five years old. It would be nearly impossible to place two dogs together that are nine and fourteen and not house-trained. I'm sorry."

"Randi, we just don't trust anyone but you with them. Could I bring them to meet you?" she begged me. "They're quite amazing."

Flattery was not going to work on me this time. No bribery could get me to take in nine- and fourteen-year-old untrained, biting rodents! I didn't want to get this woman's unrealistic hopes up more than they already were. "Look, you can stop by my adoptions this Saturday at Pet-Xtra in Tarzana, but come at the end of the day when it's slower. I can look at them, but I really don't want you to waste your time. I won't be able to take them from you. Maybe I can help you with advertising and screening potential new homes. But I can't guarantee how long it might take to find a permanent home for them. It's up to you. I don't mind meeting them."

"Thank you so much, Randi. You won't be let down once you see how cute they are. I'll see you Saturday," the woman enthusiastically said.

I was less than enthused and hoped that she would forget to come on Saturday. I don't want to mislead people, and I prayed that this woman would join the ranks of the many no-shows who did not honor their word. In this particular instance, I would welcome such irresponsibility.

But, in the back of my mind, the smiling faces of the Trocker family adopting Mindy and Cody kept appearing, and because of that, I felt motivated to figure out some way to help this woman and her geriatric rodents.

This was a very interesting time in my life. I had recently acquired my only other passion since I started rescuing dogs—magnets. Yes, everyone thought I was crazy, but I had been at a health expo several months prior to this and was intrigued by what appeared to be overinflated claims of what magnets could do for the body.

My lifelong aversion to sleep, unshakable body-building habit, and the chaotic dance of running an active dog rescue agency finally had caught up with me. As I was strolling through the hundreds of booths at this health show with a friend, Cari, who had adopted her dogs from me, I was searching for the magic cure to end all of my ailments.

At only thirty-three, I was beginning to be haunted by bleak visions of myself in my nineties, crippled with body-building injuries and poverty-stricken from the dog rescue. My great-grandfather, Benjamin Sherman, lived to 114 in Toronto, Canada, and I dreaded the thought of being blessed with his longevity. I had already weakened my knees from pushing far too much weight at the gym, had a two-year-old chronic shoulder injury from weight-lifting, and was becoming very accustomed to living with bronchitis.

While Cari ran off to have a reading with her favorite clairvoyant, John Edward, I stood at a booth rolling magnetic balls on my shoulder. Over an hour later, when Cari found me still standing at the magnetic ball booth and tried pulling me away, I said, almost in a trance, "Cari, I can't believe it. I don't even care if this is voodoo. My shoulder is better. Why didn't any of my doctors, chiropractors, or physical therapists tell me about this? No one at Gold's Gym knows about it. I was ready to have surgery on my shoulder, and now it feels better than it has in two years. The world needs to know about this."

Cari eventually dragged me away from the magnet booth, going on and on about her reading with John Edward, while my mind began going through all of the world's ailments that magnets could fix.

I never thought anything would ever evoke as much passion from me as rescuing dogs. But after a few months of sleeping on magnets, wearing them on my shoulder and knees, and using them on dogs with arthritis and nerve damage, I was sold. I felt better than ever before in my life. I was now pushing even more weights than I had ever been able to. My knees and shoulders were feeling perfect. When I hit my bed I went into a welcomed "coma." Many of my sick and old dogs had mind-boggling recoveries that defied modern science. I was so excited that the puppy pens at my open house dog adoptions were soon decorated with big pink signs that read in black lettering: "ASK US WHY OUR DOGS SLEEP ON MAGNETS" and "USING MAGNETS CAN BE HAZARDOUS TO YOUR DOCTOR'S WEALTH!"

I was now traveling the country, preaching the word about magnets as a consultant for a huge Japanese company, Nikken, while still running my dog rescue agency. My multitasking skills were at their finest, and for the first time in nine years, I was semi-comfortable delegating some of my weekend adoptions to another person, David Roe.

David and I spent over a month talking on the phone in March of the previous year before ever meeting in person. He had been fundraising for another animal rescue agency, Best Friends Animal Sanctuary. David's wacky sense of humor, partnered with one of the most beautiful soothing voices I had ever heard on the phone, created many all-night conversations between us. I had no desire ever to meet him in person. But the gentle persistence of his soothing voice convinced me that we should do so. We finally met during a rainstorm, when I was always my most invigorated and outgoing. David was horribly shy, and our anxiety over finally meeting seemed to be very much in alignment.

As I walked in the rain through the Town & Country Outdoor Shopping Center in Encino and my eyes met with what looked like one of my long-lost, Rainbow Gathering brothers, it felt as if the greatest summer of my life had just returned. We were coincidentally wearing matching overalls, and David's waist-length, curly, thick blond locks were so magnificent that they put my long, wavy, red mane to shame.

When David excitedly walked me out to his tattered 1977, bright yellow Toyota Celica hatchback and proudly introduced me to his beloved rescued dogs, Leon—an old, manic cattle dog mix—and Bear—an oversized, musty-smelling, grumpy red chow with crusty eyes—I knew this kinship would be eternal.

David had no shame in driving a less-than-impressive vehicle. As we stood in the parking lot talking and enjoying the rain, surrounded by sparkling new BMWs, Jaguars, and Mercedes (after all, this was Encino), David said, very matter of factly, "I know all of these other cars may look nice, but none of them are collector's items. You don't see many of these high quality vehicles (as he caressed the dented hood of his car) around anymore."

Many people would run from Leon and Bear, but to David, his boys were also rare treasures. It didn't take long for David to become a part of my family, and my mom embraced him as if he were her own son. He honored and respected animals in the way that my mom and I did, and in no time at all I had his small apartment stuffed full of homeless dogs.

David was one of those people who could not vocalize the word "no." He would think it, but he just couldn't bring himself to say it. This would soon change after spending some time around me, but for now, he was so very much like my mom, and I felt as if he was destined to be a forever-brother.

David constantly ran around helping anyone and anything that needed him. He was the exact person I knew I could manipulate into taking the geriatric rodents. He would feel sorry for them.

I was so swamped that, by the weekend, I had completely forgotten about the dachshunds. Adoptions that Saturday were also unusually busy, and at about 5 p.m., when I was starting to pack up everything to go home, my luck failed me. A lady came walking up to me, smiling, carrying a small wicker basket with only one "rodent" in it and what looked like a beak sticking out. I figured the ancient one had died since we had spoken, but the woman put the basket on the ground, clapped her hands and said, "Heidi! Wake up! Come out and meet Randi!"

Another "beak" emerged from under the blanket. This one looked like a fossil I might find in my garage—one eye completely white, a gray beak resembling a witch's hooked nose, and huge warts with long pieces of thick hair growing out of them. Heidi looked as if she couldn't be bothered with any of this and went back into her own little world under her blanket. In my bizarre way, I was actually curious about this one. Heidi was hideous beyond words, and I really wanted another peek at her. But she was already done with me. The woman tried to get her to come back out from under the blanket, but she would have nothing of it, and tried to bite at us while grumbling from under her blanket, "Leave me alone." Meanwhile, Pepper, although nine years old, was quite active and seemed like a normal dog, except for the unfortunate fact that, to me, she looked like a rodent. I told the woman, with as much sincerity as I could conjure up, "Yep, they sure are cute. Let me see if I can get another rescue to help you with them."

I must have gone unconscious because, within the week, somehow or another, I was the one who had been manipulated into having two "rodents" at my house. How could such a travesty have occurred at this overly hectic time in my life? What happened to David?

Fortunately, the dogs seemed to be self-contained and were very happy to be on their own with their squeaky toys. As their mother said, they spent most of their time in their basket together, chatting away about life or simply sleeping. Since they were the first dachshunds I'd ever had, I kept them separate from the other dogs, letting them out in the yard for their own private enjoyment. I was astonished as I watched the ratlike mother and daughter step off into my pool to float around and wade in it together as if they had done this frequently in the past. None of the other dogs I'd ever had would even go near my pool, but

The magnificent Heidi

now I was being peculiarly entertained by what appeared to be two miniature seals!

I knew when they arose by the sound of their squeaky toys coming alive. The mom, Heidi, the smaller of the two, weighed in at only seven pounds. She enjoyed sitting on my foot and basking in the sun when I had them outside. Pepper began running around on her own and getting into trouble.

As some time passed and I realized my two new girls weren't carrying any rodent-prone diseases, I began to integrate them with the others. Pepper was far too active for all of us. I was constantly getting her out of trouble: out of the dishwasher or trash cans, down from trees where she would attempt to climb to get to the birds and squirrels, and so on. I was exhausted just watching her.

Heidi seemed to come out of her shell the more her daughter was away from her. I suddenly realized that Heidi had been completely intimidated by her daughter, who had always been stealing her food and toys, dominating her into submission. Heidi spent most of her time hiding under her blanket to get away from the one she had given birth to nine years earlier. As David and I observed the dynamics between Heidi and Pepper, we both agreed that we should give them a trial separation. He took Pepper, who was so busy causing trouble and loving this new adventure that she didn't even notice the change.

Heidi began to blossom, coming out of her shell even more, and asked to be held often. She found much pleasure in her new life, under the covers, now sleeping next to a human. The presence of this "rodent" was becoming strangely addictive to me. I caught myself yearning to hold her and kiss the little "beak" that once repulsed me. Heidi was actually very sweet and was only snappy if someone grabbed at her before speaking, startling her due to her lack of vision.

Pepper needed her own home and was adopted shortly thereafter by a dachshund fanatic. Neither Heidi nor Pepper seemed to miss each other at all.

Several more weeks had passed when David was visiting with a few of his dogs. We were all out in the yard, watching them play. After about a half an hour, one of his bigger dogs, a ninety-pound shepherd mix, who had always been fine with the others, trotted over to Heidi and picked her up, shaking her like a rag doll. She had Heidi by the

Heidi leading the pack!

neck and wouldn't let go. Heidi gasped for air while David frantically tried to pry her loose from this dog's mouth. The dogs bit him during the rescue, but he remained so focused on saving Heidi's life, he didn't even realize it.

Finally we got Heidi loose, and as we rushed her, mouth and tongue turning blue, to the vet, I realized how attached I had become to this little girl. I was not prepared to see her life end. Heidi's neck had been ripped open, her esophagus was torn, and her heart and lungs were displaced.

Given Heidi's advanced age, my vet, Dr. Deborah Hoffman, explained she had only a five percent chance of survival. "Randi, you need to decide quickly if we should even begin to attempt to save her."

"Treat her as if she were one of your own," I said. "Do whatever you need to keep her alive, but I don't want her suffering." David was without words.

Amazingly, Heidi survived the surgery. The next several days were equally critical with the possibility of her dying due to air blockages. There was also a strong possibility that she might not be able ever again to swallow food.

When I brought Heidi home, I placed magnets under her bandages, around her neck and chest, and put a magnetic pad in the crate where she needed to be isolated. All we could do now was patiently wait and see whether she would live or die.

Heidi shocked all of us and, within only two days, was demanding food in that way dachshunds do, almost removing my fingers when I was handing out treats. Within the week, she began trotting around the house and the following week, she resumed killing her toys. My little "rodent" seemed quickly to have forgotten her gruesome brush with death.

As the weeks passed, Heidi took over the house, the other dogs, and my heart. Heidi, all seven pounds of her, became dominant over a pack of dogs who each weighed two to seven times more than she did. I celebrated her will, tenacity, and life for the five remaining years that I was honored by her strength.

Several times when driving, I've almost run off the road watching dachshunds marching their people down the street. I now understand the obsession anyone who has ever been honored to be owned by a dachshund continues to have. This is an addictive species!

CHAPTER 13

THE BEDAZZLING BUGGAR
Summer of 1996

C ross-eyed, bucktoothed, knock-kneed, and broken-tailed. I
was staring into the eyes of what was soon to become the new
man of my dreams.

Kennel cough was no longer a foreign experience for me and was
often an extra little "bonus" that came with rescuing shelter dogs. Treating it had become second nature to me. My permanent pack had been
exposed to kennel cough so often that they had all built up immunities
to it, but for the dogs coming out of the shelter with weakened immune
systems, it could attack the respiratory functions so severely that pneu-
monia would sometimes develop. One of my new rescues from the
Ventura County Animal Shelter, a mid-sized male, muddy gray-colored
mutt was in that category. His uncontrollable hacking would have terrified the many skittish rescues in my care or at least deprived everyone,
especially my mom, of any sleep. So I retreated to the opposite end of
the house where my new rescue and I camped out in the den/dog bedroom with a vaporizer next to the bed to help clear out his lungs.

This room had already been "possessed" by hundreds of new rescues before I had exorcised the demons out of them. The evidence of such occurrences was beyond anything that I could even attempt to hide. Most of the moldings along the doors had been torn off, and what little pieces did remain were strategically decorated with puncture holes from the teeth of possessed dogs. The cork floor that was a sacred antique to my mom now looked like a neglected, fifty-year old ice-skating rink. But I defended my lived-in, down-home, country-cabin style dog room as being priceless, with original décor that could never be replicated. My mom didn't debate me too much on that one, thank God.

In the back of my mind, I had fleeting thoughts of one day restoring her sacred den back to its original condition—just as soon as I stopped rescuing dogs.

This was another one that truly was a rescue. Even if I did get his kennel cough cleared up, the reality was that he would probably end up with me. As skilled as I thought I had become as a dog matchmaker, I had yet to be able easily to convince people that the middle-aged, cross-eyed, bucktoothed, knock-kneed ones were a rare score. Finding a dog with all of those characteristics was no easy task, so in my mind, the most valuable. No one seemed to agree with me.

I instantly bonded with my new rescue and, on our first night together, gave him my undivided attention. He didn't seem to mind that the bed we were sharing had an enormous sinkhole in the middle of it from one of the possessed dogs who had used it as a chew toy.

As I was kissing the head of my new rescue and holding him, I thought that my sleep deprivation had once again reached its peak, affecting my vision. The fur on his head and ears appeared to be moving. I kept blinking and then held my stare on his head long enough to realize that it was not sleep deprivation. There was a small colony of almost microscopic creatures crawling on my new dog's head.

On the nine-year anniversary of starting my rescue, I was given the gift of an entire new experience. I thought I had already lived through pretty much anything that any rescuer could share with the world, but cuddling in bed with a dog infested with lice was a first!

"Oh no! Will I have to shave off my long, thick red hair?" I thought to myself. I had done almost everything for the sake of unwanted and neglected dogs. But shaving my head was the one thing I was unwilling

to do. This was ego preservation for me, and all of a sudden my attachment to my new dog quickly ended. As I rushed out of the room to
call my twenty-four-hour vet for more information, the name "Buggar"
came to me.

"Hi, Randi. What's going on?" the familiar voice of the woman
working graveyard asked. I had become a regular at Beverly Oaks Animal Hospital, but not during regular hours. Two to 4 a.m. seemed to
be my prime time with dog issues that I was unable to treat on my own.
My mom's house had been turned into a pet infirmary. Bags of subcutaneous fluids were hanging from the outside of her kitchen cupboards.
Every ear and eye medication you could imagine had taken over her
kitchen sink. Antibiotics from A to Z were mixed in with her condi-
ments, and in the egg section of her refrigerator, now sat vaccinations
and insulin. There wasn't much that I hadn't been exposed to in regard
to pet ailments, and it made more sense to learn to care for as much of it
as possible on my own than spend even more time at the vet's offices.

"Lice aren't a life or death situation. If you want to run this rescue in,
we can have the vet take a quick look at him," the receptionist offered.

"But I'm not sure it is lice. If it is, can I get whatever I need to treat
it tonight?" I asked. "How easy is it for other dogs to catch it? I have
eight others here now, but I've kept this one separated because he also
has raging kennel cough."

My proactive nature made me always prefer immediately to take
care of any issues in lieu of sleeping.

"You should be okay," the receptionist comforted me. "We're not
that busy right now if you want to come in."

One would think that at 2:30 a.m. it wouldn't be busy anywhere.
But Beverly Oaks Emergency Animal Hospital was often the happening
place to be in the middle of the night. It had become my home away
from home, and I had learned that in the 20 minutes that it would take
for me to get there after phoning, multiple emergencies could come in
stretching my visits out for several hours. I generally was not a person
who had a high tolerance for waiting hours at any appointment, but this
phase of my life had taught me a much needed lesson in patience and
the priceless skill of learning to flow with whatever came my way.

People rushing in with comatose stray dogs that had, without warning, appeared in front of their vehicles on main intersections was a fairly

common sight during these hours. My head-lice paled in comparison as an emergency status, but the people working the graveyard shift at Beverly Oaks Animal Hospital always did their best to accommodate me.

My relationship with Buggar was off to a rocky start, but as I went back in the den to retrieve him, he was sitting on the bed staring at the door, waiting for my return, with his tail wagging, bottom teeth so misaligned that no orthodonture treatments could ever help, and his eyes still as crossed as could be. I melted from such bedazzlement. Clearly he had no clue as to how he looked.

As I went to pick him up, he coughed a big spray of phlegm into my face. All I could do was kiss his nose. Normally I would pity a dog in this state (and with these looks), but Buggar was as happy as a clam.

The ride to the vet gave us more time to bond, and Buggar seemed to be enamored with me now too. He sat beside me the entire drive, never taking his crossed eyes off me, bottom buckteeth protruding in air, and his tail expressing his thrill over our first date. I had a difficult time driving. This guy mesmerized me, and all I wanted to do was stare back at him. I wondered what, if anything, was going on in his little lice-infested head.

When we arrived at the vet's office, I breathed a sigh of relief over the sight of an empty waiting area. We immediately were put into a room with the on-call vet, who looked as though he had just gotten out of bed. He had a gentle essence about him and was of East Indian descent. He had tufts of jet black hair sticking straight up and bags under his red eyes.

"What do we have here?" he slowly asked while yawning.

"Buggar," I quickly replied.

This seemed to put a little spring in the doctor's step, waking him up a bit.

"A what?" he asked again.

"Buggar. I just named him Buggar." I really didn't want to go into much detail. I just wanted to get rid of the lice and go home. This vet was in his own world anyway and never made eye contact with me, which, on this occasion, was fine.

As he was examining Buggar, he kept telling me things that I already knew and had accepted about him.

"You know, he has a broken tail," the vet informed me.

"I do," I said. "I think it's cute. But what about the lice?"

"There's nothing that is done for broken tails," the vet went on, "and it doesn't cause the dog any pain." He ignored my comment about the lice.

While pulling back on Buggar's rear legs he then said, "Oh, he has bad luxating patellas!"

"I know," I said. "I call it knock-kneed, and I think it's even cuter than the broken tail. What about the lice?"

He started examining Buggar's head, and before he even got to his eyes, I jumped in, "I know his eyes cross a little too. Isn't he one of the cutest dogs you've ever seen?"

The vet responded with, "It looks as if he has lice. This is easily treated with a shampoo. You bathe him once tonight and then in a week."

"Is it contagious to humans?" I finally asked.

"No—there is no threat to humans catching it from a dog."

"Yes!"

My on-call vet briefly replaced Buggar's role as the new man of my dreams. A bald head was not in my future.

After nursing epileptic dogs through grand mal seizures, senior dogs in kidney and liver failure, young dogs with Parvo and distemper, calcium-deficient nursing mothers abandoned without their puppies, anemic dogs from flea-infestations, dogs riddled with cancer, and dogs with mange and ringworm, treating lice was a breeze.

By 5 a.m. Buggar and I were home, bathed, lice-free, and ready to crawl back into bed together on our freshly laundered linens. My mom and the other dogs slept through the entire evening, but now Buggar's kennel cough started acting up, and there was no way either of us could sleep through it. I had already medicated him for it, so I now had to call the emergency vet again to see if I could increase his dosage of Tussigon, which suppresses the cough. I was given the okay to do so, and by 6 a.m., Buggar and I finally drifted off to sleep.

But, at a little before 8 a.m., I could hear the other dogs in the kitchen shuffling about with my mom. Even with ear plugs in, my maternal instincts would always wake me up if I believed a dog needed me for anything. As exhausted as I was, my inclination was to get up and go check on everyone. All was fine except eight other dogs now wanted to talk to me, have some breakfast, and find out what I was hiding from them at the other end of the house. I put on my headset and started answering and returning phone calls while taking care of the others. Before I knew it, the day was gone and Buggar had slept through most of it. I periodically went to check on him and kiss his bottom buckteeth.

After almost two weeks, Buggar's kennel cough was cleared up and he was no longer contagious with anything. I couldn't wait to integrate him with the others, and they couldn't wait to meet the phantom dog that they were beginning to think I was lying to them about. As expected, Buggar loved everyone and was overjoyed finally to have a family other than me.

I began bringing Buggar to my adoptions, but no bows, colognes, or fancy dog sweaters did the trick to draw admirers to him. Nevertheless, he was still as happy as a clam and wagged his tail at everyone who laughed at his looks. My intention has always been to rescue and rehome unwanted dogs, not keep them permanently. And really, Buggar had no issues that would justify my keeping him. He was as perfect as a dog could be. He loved everyone and everything, was house-trained, and was truly an enjoyable energy to have around. My salesman skills would now have to be fine-tuned for Buggar's sake. He deserved his own person.

I realized that I would have to "sell" Buggar on the phone to someone so that they would already be in love with him before they met him. A woman in her early 70s, Elaine, would be the perfect candidate. Elaine wanted me to select a dog for her because she had no preferences other than it be a small to medium sized adult and house-trained.

"I like a dog with a little bit of chutzpah and character," Elaine said during our first conversation. "I would take my dog with me whenever I go anywhere, and the rest of the time he would be home with me. When can I come to meet all of your dogs?"

"Well," I replied, "I can only think of one who seems to fit all of your requirements."

The truth was that Elaine didn't have as rigid requirements as most of the people wanting to adopt from my rescue. Some of the other dogs were far more desirable than Buggar: smaller, younger, and more striking in the superficial looks department. But none had the chutzpah of Buggar. Before I finished telling Elaine about all of Buggar's unique qualities, she interrupted me, saying, "When can I come get my dog? I'm lonely and I'm ready for him now."

Nine years of placing thousands of dogs may have transformed me into the world's greatest salesman. I had sold Elaine on my Buggar!

I decided to meet Elaine privately at a small pet shop on Ventura Boulevard near her home the following Friday afternoon. I also had to begin preparing myself emotionally to release the man of my dreams, knowing that it was for his highest good.

As I was trying to convince myself that this was the right thing to do, I decided that there were some other things that were a plus about Elaine. She lived close to me, and she said that she had gone to my long-time vet at Tarzana Pet Clinic with her pets that had passed away. I would be able to keep close tabs on Elaine and Buggar through Dr. Hoffman.

I made it through the week and was awaiting Elaine's arrival at the pet shop. A part of me was hoping she wouldn't show up or would be so late that I could justify sneaking off to prolong this parting. But I caught myself in these thoughts and attempted to stop my mind from creating a doomed outcome for Buggar's future.

Buggar was wagging his tail and staring at everyone who walked by. Had I let him select his own new guardian, he probably would have ended up with the neighborhood schizophrenic man who had made a habit of visiting Buggar each weekend at my adoptions. This man would clear out the crowds of potential adoptive parents when he would show up, screaming profanities about killing people and the war, just at the same time he would begin to drop his drawers. The police knew him well and escorted him off Ventura Boulevard on a regular basis with him laughing his way to jail. The second they let him out, he would run to the store to stock up on cookies for Buggar in anticipation of the weekend adoptions.

Although everyone else was in fear of this man, I found him thoroughly entertaining and appreciated the fact that Buggar had a secret admirer other than me. I actually began having some lucid conversations with this man and noticed that all of his anger would fade away as he was petting Buggar. His face would soften the more he focused on Buggar, and his other side would then emerge—a gentle, smiling, coherent man, who had the potential of being a valuable member of society. Buggar found nothing wrong with this man, and he was one of the only people who reciprocated Buggar's unconditionally accepting ways. There was definitely a connection developing between the two, and it actually hurt me as I would watch the man tear himself away from Buggar, aware enough to admit that he spent too much time in jail to take Buggar on as a full-time pet.

As I awaited Elaine's arrival, my hyperactive mind began to worry about this man's only joy being taken away from his weekend outings at my adoptions. Buggar was the only one with whom he seemed to have that special connection, and I wondered if losing those visitation rights would permanently send him off the deep end.

But my train of thought took an abrupt turn when it seemed as though I had been transported to the movie set of the classic film, *Sunset Boulevard*. Gloria Swanson appeared to be making a grand entrance toward me and my Buggar. With her arms outstretched and gait as theatrical as one could imagine, "Gloria" slowly waltzed up to us, singing, "Is this my Buggar?" Elaine had just arrived and was on time.

Maybe even more eccentric than Buggar's schizophrenic admirer, one quick glance of Elaine gave me relief in seeing that no ordinary dog would do. Elaine was in a world of her own making. As she took Buggar's leash from my hand, she very softly but directly gave me her instructions. "Randi, I want you to follow us to my house. I'll stop at my pet store and get food on the way home." I didn't quite feel as though I was cast in Elaine's movie yet and found myself almost unable to speak. Before she sped off, I made sure she gave me her address.

Elaine disappeared and, while I was still driving, hoping to find her car, I received a call on my cell phone from one of the women working at Tarzana Pet Clinic. "Randi, there's a woman named Elaine who's waiting to meet you here. She seems confused, said you were late, and thought this was a pet shop. She has one of your dogs and said she's going home because she can't wait for you any longer."

I think I was even more confused than everyone else who had been cast in this movie. I only had Elaine's address and didn't get directions since I thought I would be following her. I went home and immediately phoned Elaine. I had no idea what I was going to say or do. I left a message on her answering machine, and she phoned back within the hour.

"Randi, I think I'm going to change his name to Snaggles, short for Snaggle-Tooth. He fits in like a glove here. We have to go now. It's time for our dinner date," and she hung up.

Speechless was an understatement. I was baffled. This was another first for me.

I gave them the night together and was going to phone the next day. Elaine hadn't even filled out any adoption paperwork but phoned me early the next day before I had a chance to figure out what I was going to say to her.

"Randi, what time are you coming over today? Snaggles and I have some plans, but we can fit you into our hectic schedule."

I also had appointments already scheduled throughout the day and had one of my volunteers get over to Elaine's house as soon as possible. Shockingly, all was going well, and Buggar seemed to have quickly forgotten who I was, settling into Elaine's home as though he had always been there. Elaine filled out all of our adoption paperwork and was now Buggar's legal guardian.

I didn't hear from Elaine for several days until she phoned to ask for help.

"Randi, do you know of someone who can come here to help me with Snaggles? I can't seem to remember if I fed him, and he has no way to get out to go to the bathroom."

The schizophrenic man came to mind, but I couldn't even begin to fathom what kind of trouble those two would get into together. I had yet to exercise my right to reclaim a dog according to the Recycled Pets adoption contract, and this option was now entering my mind as a viable solution. But I dreaded the thought of uprooting Buggar and also taking away Elaine's new companion. I arranged to have people check in on Elaine and Buggar every day. The consensus from everyone was that Elaine was very eccentric but loved Snaggles and, with a little assistance, was as good as any guardian could be. I was able to let go of worry, fear, and doubt, finally releasing Buggar completely.

Almost two years had passed when I received a message on my voice mail. "Hi, I'm a friend of Elaine's, and I think she got a dog named Snaggles from you. Could you please call me back as soon as possible?"

In the rescue world, no news is good news, so my heart skipped a beat as I dialed this woman's phone number. After a brief but in-depth conversation, it was my understanding that Buggar was being boarded because poor Elaine was now in a mental hospital with no plans of coming home.

I set up a time to have him returned to me the following day.

I barely recognized Buggar when we reconnected. It looked as though a brush, shampoo, or water hadn't touched him in months. But he definitely had not missed any meals and looked like a pregnant sheep with chopsticks for limbs. But I knew it was my Buggar because his

Buggar

rear knees were knocking together as he waddled up to me, his bottom teeth were protruding in the air, his eyes were still as crossed as could be, and his tail was wagging in circles. A two-year separation had not diminished Buggar's zest for life. With all he had gone through, he was still as happy as a clam.

The integration back into my life appeared to be a birthday party for Buggar, and I took the honor of shearing his heavily matted coat. This, too, seemed like a celebration for Buggar, and once again, he had no clue that he now looked like a miniature, cross-eyed dinosaur needing braces. Even though he was now less adoptable than when I had first rescued him, Buggar was blissfully beaming with joy.

"How could I ever place you again?" I said to him, while kissing his bottom buckteeth. "No one will ever be good enough for you." Really, Buggar was happy no matter whom he was with or where he was. The schizophrenic man came to mind again, but I hadn't seen him along Ventura Boulevard for ages now, and the pet shop, where I had shown Buggar at my open house adoptions, had gone out of business.

Several weeks later, just as I was resigned to keeping Buggar, I received the phone call for which I had been hoping.

One of my favorite adoptive moms from my earlier rescue days had taken on two of my not-very-adoptable rescues about eight years previously. One of the dogs had such severe skin problems that I intervened on his behalf just before the owners were considering euthanasia. Janice, who was from England, felt like one of my moms from a past life the second I spoke to her on the phone. Upon our first meeting, I knew that this was someone I would want to keep in my life beyond this adoption. She exuded that warm and safe feeling, which one would think babies experience while in their mothers' wombs. I knew that with Janice, these two unadoptables would be safe and cared for over the long haul.

Now, almost eight years later, Janice's daughter, who was living alone, was looking to adopt her own dog. Christina was a sweetheart, was in her early 20s, and like her mom, was open to taking on a less-desirable rescue. I gave her no option. Buggar had her name written all over him. Christina was as easy as her mom, who accompanied her on this first rendezvous. They were eager to meet my now almost-famous Buggar, but not as much as I was to reconnect with them and finally have Buggar in one home for the rest of his life.

I'll never forget the laughs and smiles that he brought out of them as they rushed toward us upon our meeting. Buggar was in love, but then again, it wasn't personal—Buggar loved anything that moved. This adoption was as easy as when Janice had adopted her "kids" from me years earlier, and Christina went home with my Buggar. My heart was finally at peace.

We spoke daily, and Christina relayed to me what I already knew—Buggar was as easy as could be, fitting in as though they had always been together. Once again, from the moment his leash left my hand and was in Christina's, he forgot I existed. Out of sight, out of mind was Buggar's philosophy. He lived in the moment and maybe was one of the world's most evolved beings. I wished all of my rescues acclimated to change as smoothly as Buggar did.

During my next conversation with Christina, she mentioned she had seen on some of the paperwork that came with Buggar that his name had also been Snaggles. She preferred to call him Snaggles, which was fine with me. My Buggar responded to any name or words. He would have been just as happy with sign language too!

In that same conversation, Christina expressed her desire to get a sibling for my Buggar. She thought he would be even happier with a little sister.

Shortly afterwards, we had another glorious reunion, and Buggar and Christina went home with a perfect little girl Lhasa mix named Wickett. Again, the transition for everyone was as easy as could be. In my last conversation with Christina, she let me know that they were one happy family, living as though they had always been together.

But, the following year, my rescue woes were brought to their peak. Christina phoned, telling me that she had to return both Buggar and Wickett. She was now married, and her life had taken a different course. I had a waiting list of people wanting to adopt small, female, trained, fluffy, perfect dogs. But there was no one eager to adopt a cross-eyed, bucktoothed, knock-kneed, middle-aged dog.

Wickett went directly into a new forever home, and Buggar came back to me for his last time. My heart ached over the karma that he was dealt in this lifetime. Upon rekindling my relationship with Buggar, I saw that he held no resentment toward anyone. Buggar, like always, was as happy as a clam. His attitude immediately eased my rescue woes. He hadn't an ounce of sadness or pain over his karma. I seemed to be the only one who was suffering. Buggar was helping me to understand better the concept that everything is always in Divine Right Order, no matter how things may appear.

Every time Buggar was returned to me, the gift of his positive attitude made me more deeply attached to him. But Buggar would help me with this issue too. He had no attachments to anything, which was why he was always radiating rapture. Now I released all fear about Buggar's past, present, or future karma. This was energy that could be spent in other places. Worrying about Buggar served no purpose, and he now convinced me that whatever path his life would take was fine with him. If need be, I was also more than glad to be his forever mom.

Not much time passed before I received a phone call from Betty Kramer. She and her husband, Rabbi Bill Kramer, were hoping I could find them a dog that would be a good match for their leisurely, retired lifestyle. They preferred an older, calm male that would sit with Rabbi Bill, who was ambulatory only with a walker. I had mentally scratched my Buggar off my list of our Recycled Pets that were available for adoption. But, as I described the ones I thought would fit into their household, Betty kept passing each one over, asking about any others.

"I go to the shelters at least once a week, and I can keep my eyes open for someone that might work for you," I offered Betty. "But I guess I'm not quite sure what you're looking for. I have several right now that are calm and trained that I already mentioned to you."

"Do you have any older than the ones you mentioned?" Betty asked. "I'm afraid that the ones you told me about would be too active for us."

Rarely did anyone request a dog over five years old. In the rescue world, this was not desirable, even for senior citizens. This was frustrating to my volunteers and me because if seniors weren't willing to adopt a mature adult, which would be the most appropriate match, who would? Because of this, the senior rescues were often cast aside and left behind. This is when the bleeding heart volunteers (including me) would end up stepping in, making them a permanent part of our families. And it seemed that these rescues would always outlive the ones that were adopted by the many people who stated "I just can't handle having one die on me that soon. I need to have a dog less than three years old."

Both Sarah, my long-time volunteer, and I had our houses full of these mature unadoptables, and some had surpassed voting age.

So when Betty gently pleaded with me to search for a mature, wise companion to sit by her husband and complete their home, I felt inclined to fill Betty and Rabbi Bill in on Buggar's story. Betty was instantly convinced that they were divinely guided to meet Buggar. Now, with my new understanding about detachment, I agreed to set a time for all of us to meet.

Since most of the pet shops near me had gone out of business, I was now meeting prospective dog parents at one of my vet's offices near my house. This time I was neither eager nor anxious and had no attachment to the outcome. I was simply meeting Rabbi Bill and Betty, looking forward to such an honor, as he was a well-known icon in the Jewish community.

Over the next several days, I didn't put much energy into the possibility of once again releasing Buggar. The time quickly flashed by, being filled with answering and returning phone calls, caring for my other rescues, running to vets, and meeting with prospective pet parents.

Before I knew it, Betty and I were sitting together, laughing while watching Buggar, who was sitting against Rabbi Bill's walker staring up at him. They looked like fraternal twins that had just been reunited. Both Rabbi Bill and Buggar were distinguished in their own rights, had long gray beards, and emitted a contented wisdom about them for which no words could do justice. As Betty was giggling, she quietly whispered to me, "Randi, I can't believe it. They look exactly alike! I've never seen a dog that looked just like my husband."

Buggar's leash slipped away from me for the last time, being clutched in the hands of the rabbi. Buggar instantly gravitated to Rabbi Bill and seemed to know that his purpose was to make the rabbi smile for the last few years he would spend here.

Buggar lived out the rest of his life with Betty after the rabbi passed on. Buggar enjoyed his entire journey here, never labeling any of it as bad. His presence in my life gave me some of the greatest training that I would ever experience throughout my rescue years. He taught me that when we detach from an expected outcome, releasing worry, fear, and doubt, we allow the doors to open for the highest and best universal good to come easily shining through. Rabbi Bill and Buggar...may you rest together in bliss!

CHAPTER 14

MUNCHKIN AND ROXY
April 4, 1999

"We want that one!" yelled a desperate voice from my left.

"But we were here first, and we also want that one!" a New York accent screeched from behind me, out of a Mercedes Benz window.

"But my dog just died last week, and that one reminds me of her," moped a pouty-faced, young boy, tugging at my blue jeans that as always were laced in a rainbow of dog hair.

Chaos had struck at Martex Pet Shop in Encino. Not the sort of chaos I suppose anyone would be familiar with but me. It wouldn't be until seven years later that I would understand this day was the first part of the universe's divine way of utilizing dogs to connect me with those rare humans my heart could not do without.

Twenty-two years earlier, I had stood here in the same, charming, quaint pet shop, conversing with Lucky and Skippy about which treats they wanted for the day. The only thing that hadn't changed in that time was the stifling heat that came with Valley summers and my fair-skinned body's sensitivity to it. Ten minutes in the heat of a summer's day and

I was almost certain to be battling throbbing temples and beet-red skin that matched the color of my long, red braids.

But there was nothing in the world that I looked forward to more than my summer walks with Lucky and Skippy around the corner to Martex Pet Shop to reward them for being the best friends I had ever known. There was not much room in my life for any humans. Lucky and Skippy filled every yearning I ever had for companionship, and our conversations made more sense and were much deeper than anything I had ever experienced with any human of any age in my very important first eight years of life.

When Martex Pet Shop closed its doors years later, it felt as if my childhood was stripped away from me. "Such an injustice to the three of us," I complained to Lucky and Skippy while searching for four-leaf clovers under our plum tree in our backyard. "How can I ever make this up to you?"

It wasn't until years later, after Lucky died and Skippy was tragically hit by a car, that I would come to understand a concept I had never before experienced—regret. I had always charged ahead in life, not looking back. But seeing Skippy at fourteen and crippled from the impact of a car hitting his already feeble body changed all of that. My thoughts instantly took me back to everything he and Lucky had given me in my childhood. They gave me a reason to be and the irreplaceable, unconditional friendship that I felt could only come from the superior soul of a dog.

As I carried Skippy out of the animal shelter that day, I realized that I had not returned to Lucky and Skippy even a fraction of all that they had given me. Both of them had been more than eager to continue giving all of themselves to me. But I became preoccupied with other things. Lucky and Skippy spent the second half of their lives at the bottom of my list of priorities. I hoped to be aware enough so that never again would I create a situation causing me to live with regret.

The souls of Lucky and Skippy seemed to forgive me for my humanness, and with the birth of Recycled Pets, they began to let me know that they were still here with me. They continued to speak to me, and one day I thought I heard them saying, "Mom, regret is only a negative human concept that you guys create in your mind—or not. We dogs don't know anything about such negative things."

With my newfound awareness of living without regret, and now with many new dogs in my life, my pleasurable walks through Encino resumed. But now a tad bit of obedience work was thrown into the walks. Snickers, Skooter, Buster, and Rooney would take turns practicing "sit," "stay," "down," and "come." All of them, except one, did an impressive job of it. The one who didn't respond to any of my commands was, of course, my son Rooney. Rooney was entirely bored with all of this and was constantly on the lookout for whatever mischief he could get into. But I was determined at least to get this little troublemaker to sit.

Rooney needed lots of action around him; the more distractions, the better. I tried to bargain with him and said, "Come on, if we practice on Ventura Boulevard, where you have more than enough stimuli to entertain you, will you please at least just sit for three seconds? I'll take you to Fromin's Deli afterwards."

There was no bargaining with Rooney but in an attempt to maintain my "alpha" status with my spoiled son, I still put in the effort. He thought "sit" meant "sit up and beg extra cute." To Rooney, "stay" meant "run off and chase the first man who walks by." In Rooney's dictionary, "down" meant "punch Mom in the face and nip at her nose." He thought he was the most darling angel in the history of all life, and I couldn't get frustrated with him since I was the only person who agreed with him.

On this one particular night, Rooney and I were attempting to practice our obedience exercises in front of some stores on Ventura Boulevard that were already closed. I never took Rooney off his leash for even a second because it was a sure thing that he would disappear faster than the speed of light. Had he not been leashed this evening, a man's leg would have been bitten. I jumped back when he started barking and lunging at the male half of a couple who came out from one of the dark, closed stores.

"We've been watching you," the man said. "You're really good. Are you a dog trainer?"

"Are you kidding?" I said. "This is the most incorrigible brat I've ever tried to train. He won't even hold a sit-stay for a second."

"But you're so patient with him."

Rooney had stopped barking and was now staring at me, sitting up and begging, which meant "pick me up, Mom," so, of course, I did. He wrapped his legs around my waist, threw his forepaws around my neck, stared at me, and then nipped at my nose when I said, "I have to be. He's my son. Who else would put up with him? I thought all of the stores here were already closed."

"Yeah," the man said. "We're just opening a pet shop here, and we're still getting everything set up."

"Oh my God! That's awesome! I rescue dogs and live just around the corner," I squealed.

The woman enthusiastically said, "I had a pet shop here years ago that I closed down. You might remember it if you live around the corner."

"No way! I was always at that pet shop with my dogs, Lucky and Skippy. I walked them there every weekend and let them pick out their treats. Was it exactly in this spot?" I asked in disbelief.

The woman stared at me in a strange way and then asked, "Did you used to wear your hair in long braids?"

"Yes!"

"I remember you and your dogs. You look exactly the same. My name is Susan. What's your name?"

"Randi," I said. "We were so depressed when you closed your store. You always gave my dogs treats and didn't charge us. We had nowhere to walk to without your store here. I can't believe you're coming back."

Susan, with the biggest grin on her face, said, "This is Bill."

Bill looked like an overgrown little boy and was wearing a baseball hat backward. He seemed to be even more excited than we were over this conversation and said, "You come and see us any time and bring all of your dogs."

"That would be kind of difficult," I replied. "I recently started my rescue and always have more dogs than I can count."

Susan's enthusiasm was quickly escalating. "You could bring all of your dogs here for people to meet. We can make room in the store or in front of it for you. We'll even put up signs for you."

"Wow!" I said. "That's an amazing idea. I've mostly been placing my dogs through Pet Orphans Fund's weekend adoptions. We would have so much exposure here."

From that night came the birth of the first open house dog adoptions along Ventura Boulevard. Between Martex Pet Shop and a Petco Pet Store in Studio City, my adoptions exploded. People would show up hours early, waiting to adopt my dogs. The demand far exceeded anything I could have imagined, and I often wasn't prepared for the large crowds who awaited my arrival.

On this adoption day in October 1992, everyone seemed to be battling it out for a little female puppy in search of a home. She must have been something spectacular because some of the interested parties were behaving less than respectably, desperate to be the "winners." I relished the fact that a discarded little terrier mix puppy was so charismatic that adults were behaving in such a fashion. But I also preferred not to have to referee such battles. Inevitably, someone would leave, uttering profanities about me and/or my rescue. Needless to say, these types of people would never withstand the rigorous screening process everyone must undergo with an adoption of this nature.

The proud new parents of this dog were young newlyweds, the only people at the adoptions that manic day who I did not have to pull away from the other interested parties. Other than the battle I described at the beginning of this chapter, this was just another one of my typical adoptions and was soon filed away in Recycled Pets' archives. Years later, I would discover that this adoption held quite a different meaning for the puppy's proud parents.

It was now April 1999, and Martex Pet Shop had again closed its doors. I was holding my adoptions at a small, privately owned pet shop in Woodland Hills, Pet Life. This was in a posh location, bordering some of the nicest gated communities in the San Fernando Valley: Hidden Hills, Calabasas, and Bell Canyon. But this was also the only location I had ever visited where people walked around the adoption dogs, avoiding them like the plague. It was all quite bizarre to me, and adoptions had slowed down like never before. The crowds of eager, potential adopters were a thing of the past as was the intense, high energy that was created from such "rallies." I longed for those days to return.

But many things had changed from the earlier years of my rescuing. I had heard that pet adoptions were now mostly conducted via the Internet. To me, nothing sounded more soulless. I didn't even own a computer and had no intentions of acquiring one. I was sure that computers were merely ploys from other planets to do away with us. How can one get a sense of people from their typing skills the way one can from the inflections in their voices or the expressions on their faces? I would still find that "dream-come-true" home for each and every one of my dogs. It might take a bit longer, but I refused to succumb to soulless computer technology, no matter how many people laughed at me.

Some other things had changed since my early years of dog rescue. Now, as one of the top magnetic health care consultants in North America, I was busy traveling in addition to running my adoptions. I spoke at meetings throughout North America, vowing to give up dog rescue so that I could fully focus on my magnet career.

I lied. Yes, rescuing dogs is an intense, passionate, and often painful path to follow. And yes, I occasionally yearn for a simpler, slow-paced, unencumbered life of luxury. And yes, magnets transformed my life as well as many dogs that were written off due to hopeless health issues. But as well-honed as I thought I was at saying, "No, I'm sorry. I can't take your dog," there would always seem to be that one that I could not turn away. So, my Bronco was now weighted down with magnetic mattresses, pillows, and balls, all covered in dog hair, from the collars, leashes, crates, dog beds, and bowls that sat beside them. I now had a two-track mind.

This particular Sunday adoption on April 4, 1999, was about the slowest one I had ever seen. Blustery Santa Ana winds were whipping through the parking lot of the mini-mall. It seemed that the few people who were in the mall were in a rush, but they were all rushing right past the cutest dogs that could ever be in need of homes. It was a hopeless adoption day, and I was preoccupied with a magnet business trip that I would be attending in Indiana the following week.

The people working at Pet Life offered to watch my dogs while I quickly ran some errands. There was a beauty supply store several doors down, and I thought I would go in and browse. Spending most of my adult life dressing like a tomboy made me appreciate now having a reason to pamper myself a bit. A manicurist was sitting in the empty store, as bored as I was at my desolate adoptions.

We smiled at each other, and she said, "You like?" as she pointed to my very dirty nails. "I do for you."

"Oh—no, no. I work with dogs. They would immediately look like this again," I tried to communicate to her.

But she nodded her head and patted the empty chair, saying, "I give you good price."

"Oh—no, no," I again said. "I have dogs out here, and I can't leave them."

"T'ank you," she said, again nodding her head while bringing out all of her manicuring supplies and pulling out the chair for me.

She had trapped me. I surrendered. This was the last thing I needed to be doing, but I figured I'd enjoy it and never again go near this store.

About twenty minutes later, still in deep manicure ritual, I heard yelling: "Randi! Randi! Randi! Where are you? We know you're in here."

Of course, the one time I decide to pamper myself, there's an emergency with a dog or maybe even all of the dogs, I thought to myself, maybe the puppy pens blew over, and all of the dogs are running through the parking lot.

I jumped out of my chair to see what had happened and was tackled by a young couple.

"Randi! We've been looking everywhere for you! Do you remember us? We were going shopping for carob chips for the cookies we're making for Munchkin, and we saw your sign, Recycled Pets. We've been looking for you for years. We adopted our daughter from you in 1992," the young woman with a face of an angel said, hugging me. "I'm Barbara, and this is my husband, Mitch. Do you remember us?"

I didn't know what to say, but that didn't matter. Both of them were talking at the same time.

"You gave us the million-dollar mutt," Mitch said. "We spent a fortune on her. Can we return her, and get all of our money back?"

Barbara laughed while playfully slapping him and said, "Mitch! Stop it!" She looked up at me and said, "He's just joking. Munchkin is our life. Every day we thank you for her, and we wanted to tell you in person. Randi, you are like God to us for letting us adopt her. There were a bunch of other people who all wanted her."

"You guys are so cute, but I barely remember you or the dog. Will you ever forgive me?" I asked. "Wait—were you the ones who got the puppy that almost caused a riot at Martex all those years ago? You must be pretty phenomenal if I picked you. Why didn't you just call me over the years?"

"Oh," Barbara said, "we know how busy you are. We didn't want to bother you. You know what? You have a dog who looks just like

Barbie and Munchkin

Munchkin. She's so cute. The people in the pet shop told us to come in here and get you. Can we hold her?"

I paid the manicurist, noticing that my nail polish was already dented, and followed Mitch and Barbara two doors down, back to the pet store.

"Which dog is it?" I asked.

They both pointed to a little, fluffy, five-month-old, multi-colored, terrier mix and said, "That one!"

I took the little Yorkie mix out of the puppy pen and handed her to Mitch and Barbara, who were holding hands like teenagers the entire time.

"Had this been the olden days of dog adoptions," I told them, "that little puppy would have caused a riot. I'm surprised I still have her after two weeks. She was dumped on the side of a highway in Camarillo, and a friend from the shelter brought her to me. She's such a good little girl, especially for being a five-month-old terrier. I rarely keep the young dogs with my own because they're usually so hyper. But she is a wise soul, and my dogs all love her. If she were old and unadoptable, I wouldn't mind keeping her."

"Oh my God, Mitch!" Barbara said. "I'm gonna cry. I love her so much."

They were both holding her at the same time as if they had just given birth. I hadn't yet named her because I thought I would have immediately placed her.

"Our spoiled little 'Satan' dog hates other dogs," Mitch said sarcastically. "We really want her to have a little sister, but I think she would try to kill it."

Mitch, Barbara and the little terrier puppy still were embracing in a group hug when Mitch said, "Barbie, I think we should let them meet. Maybe Munchkin would be okay with her because she's so young. She might even think she is related to her."

Barbie's eyes started to tear. She really had the most angelic, non-human way about her. She wasn't anything like most of the other people in this area.

Actually, neither of them were. Barbie was like a five-year-old girl, swept away in the moment. Mitch was like her protective dad, and as he wiped the tears off of her face, said, "What's wrong, Smurfy?"

Barbie all of a sudden became very coy and quietly said, while look-ing down, "Mitchy, I really think I love this little girl, but I don't want her to get hurt. I don't think we should try it."

"Smurfy," Mitch said, "I'll hold 'Satan' back on a leash so the puppy can't get hurt. Nothing will happen to her. I promise."

Barbie's face lit up and her childlike grin returned, so big that it almost stretched up to her beautiful blue eyes.

"Really?" she said. "I really want Munchkin to have a little sister. I think it would be good for her to have to learn to play and share. We really spoiled her bad, huh, Mitch? Maybe it will make her nicer."

"Yes, honey, whatever you say," Mitch said, in a condescending way while rubbing her shoulder and petting the puppy that Barbie was hold-ing like her newborn.

This couple was like none other I had ever known. I could see why I'd picked them out of a crowd to adopt their first dog.

Mitch, in his authoritarian way, said, "Okay, what do we do now?"

"Well," I said, "do you want to bring your other dog here so that they can meet on neutral territory?"

"That's not a good idea," Mitch replied, deepening his voice. "I'm not kidding you when I say she is 'Satan'."

"Well, I trust you guys to take her, but just make sure you intro-duce them outside of the house so Munchkin won't be as protective. I can come by after the adoption. If they don't get along, just keep them separate from each other until I get there."

Barbie was so excited that her eyes again began to tear. I guess Mitch was used to this because he didn't react, other than wiping away her tears.

Mitch and Barbie left with the little girl Yorkie mix. They were one of the few couples I felt I could completely trust, and I looked forward to seeing how they all fared.

I lost myself in the rest of the day, and before I knew it, 6 p.m. had already passed. I had to drop off my small group of adoption dogs at my house, since none of them had been adopted. I also had to run to an animal shelter to check on another dog.

On my way over to Mitch and Barbie's house, I called them from my cell phone, and they both answered the phone saying, "What hap-pened to you?"

"We thought you died," Mitch said. "Hurry up! We're all waiting for you."

As I drove up to their house, I was taken aback. They looked and acted like young kids playing house, but their new home was a mini-palatial estate, not the sort of place I would think of as dog friendly. It was an all-white, Mediterranean mini-mansion with high ceilings and a three-car garage. It sat at the top of a guard-gated community that must have been housing some of those many people who acted as though my dogs were carrying the plague.

Mitch and Barbie did not fit in here. They were humble, sensitive animal lovers. I bet there's another side to them, I thought to myself. I bet they're really sterile, anal-retentive, uptight people who lock their animals in one small room so as not to dirty their house. Better yet, this probably isn't even their house. They're probably pathological liars who borrowed this house for the evening only to impress me.

Barbie opened the sky-high double doors and reached out to hug me. "Randi! We missed you! What took you so long? We wanted you to have dinner with us."

Who are these people, I thought to myself. This Barbie is not human, or at least not like any human I've ever met.

"Come in," she said. "Mitch is with the girls."

As I cautiously walked into the mini-palatial estate, I heard a TV blasting, accompanied by the squawking of birds and barking of dogs. I thought I had died and been transported to a modern-day Noah's ark. I slowly followed Barbie into the huge, spacious family room.

I felt as if I was crashing a party when Mitch toasted me in the air with his glass of Johnny Walker Black Scotch. "Cheers! Can I get you a drink?"

Maybe this was really a mental institution, I thought to myself. It's a normal Sunday night and tomorrow is Monday, a workday. What are these people doing? They're acting as if it's New Year's Eve.

Their "Satan" dog, Munchkin, ran up to me barking. She indeed looked exactly like a big version of the puppy, both fluffy and multi-colored with that Benji appearance. The puppy was playing tug-of-war with a ten-foot-long scarf with Mitch tugging on the other end of it from their overstuffed, black, elegant sofa. They had a macaw parrot who squawked at me even louder than Munchkin barked, and off in

Mitch and Roxy

another corner were cockatiels who were singing away with the rest of the choir.

Munchkin finally stopped barking at me and ran off to chase the puppy, who immediately started chasing her in circles. There was no danger of anyone getting hurt here. On the contrary, this was an amusement park.

Munchkin's toys were spread out on the sofa and throughout the living room, and the two girls never stopped barking and playing while jumping on and off the furniture.

Barbie took my hand and said, "Come on upstairs. You can see our bedroom where we all sleep. Oh, by the way, Randi, do you think Roxy will sleep under the covers with us? We always try to get Munchkin to, but she won't."

I had no idea what she was talking about. Actually I had no idea where I even was, what planet I was on, or who these people were—if, in fact, they really were people.

Barbie walked me into their huge, luxurious bedroom, while still holding my hand, and said, "Here, sit on the bed with me. Oh, we forgot to tell you something. We wanted to name her after you, so we picked a name that started with an R—Roxy."

Both of the girls came bounding into the bedroom, leaping over the bed and back down the stairs, where I heard Mitch say, "Come on, my girls. You're both so cute. Daddy's your favorite, huh, Roxy?"

Barbie again hugged me while we sat on their bed, which also was covered in dog toys, and said, "Thank you so much, Randi. You'll never know how happy you made us, and how much you mean to us." Another tear cascaded down her angel face.

That evening was one I hoped would never end. It reminded me of every reason why I cannot walk away from dog rescue. And it made me believe that Lucky and Skippy truly were still talking to me. They sent Munchkin and Roxy to me to bring me Mitch and Barbara Gordon, "dream-come-true" dog parents, who soon became some of the greatest human friends I would ever treasure in this lifetime.

CHAPTER 15

NO GOOD DEED GOES
UNPUNISHED
Fall 1999

In the fall of 1999, a charming mother and daughter came to me to adopt a shih-tzu as the mother's shih-tzu had recently passed away. Upon meeting them, I could see that the daughter, who was in her forties, would be leading this search. I met them at the home of one of my foster parents to show them an adorable pair of almost pure shih-tzus with beautiful temperaments that I had for adoption. This is where this story took an unexpected turn.

The daughter fell in love with another one of my rescue dogs and adopted him, although that was not her initial intention. The mother continued looking for a purebred shih-tzu.

Several weeks later, the daughter phoned, saying, "Randi, we need your help with a shih-tzu we rescued from a shelter. He was going to be put to sleep so we took him, but my mom can't keep him. When can we bring him to you?"

I immediately knew that some pertinent information must have been omitted that I would need to know before committing to taking in this dog. I began to ask some questions.

"Wasn't your mom looking for a purebred shih-tzu? Why doesn't she want to keep him?"

"Well, she's having some problems handling him. Can you go pick him up from her house?" the daughter asked.

I had to pry a bit more in an attempt to gather the entire story and asked, "Why can't she handle him? Is he too heavy for her to lift?"

"No, but he doesn't like being picked up. Can you call my mom and set a time to go get him?"

Some people help me learn how to do my "job" even more efficiently. This was one of those situations where I felt as if I were a psychologist, peeling at an onion to get to the core of what was really going on. I had to be very specific. "What does he do that leads you to believe he doesn't like to be picked up?"

"He squirms away, and then tries to snap," she said.

Now we were getting somewhere, and I continued on. "Are you yourself able to pick him up, or perhaps both of you together?"

"We haven't really been able to, but since you're the expert, you probably wouldn't have a problem with it. Can you go get him tomorrow from my mom?" the daughter persisted. "She really needs you to come and get him as soon as possible."

Again, it seemed that this very loving and gentle mother and daughter were dodging something, but I wasn't sure what. If this dog was only snapping a bit, I would think that they would be willing to work through it.

I finally said, "If you bring him to me, I will evaluate him for you."

"That won't work," she replied. "We really need you to come and get him."

"Well, I'm swamped this whole week, and I'm really maxed out with dogs right now," I said. "I will look at him for you if you want to bring him to me."

"We can't," the daughter said.

"Why?" I responded.

This was the never-ending conversation, and I was ready to get off the phone after the first few incomplete sentences from the daughter. But I had been so very drawn to them when I had met them and appreciated how the daughter seemed to take on the parenting role with her mom, gently nurturing her through this process. If at all possible, I wanted to be able to assist them.

Still, the conversation was beginning to feel like a tortuous, tooth-pulling session when she finally said, "We can't get him in the car."

Again, I had to ask, "Why?"

"We can't lift him without getting bitten. He was turned into the shelter by his owners, and they had him listed as a biter. But he was so cute, we felt we would do a good deed and save his life. He at least deserves that," she said. "Don't you agree?"

I spent the next half-hour coaching the daughter on how to get the dog into a crate and into the car without them getting bitten so that they could transport him. I wasn't yet convinced that I even wanted to meet this dog. Temperament has always been a first priority to me; cuteness came in a distant second.

The mom had already been bitten several times, and the bites did break her skin. But the daughter persisted: "Randi, I bet this dog has been abused, which is why he's biting. You'll be able to help him. I'm sure of it. If we can get him in the car, can we bring him to you tomorrow?"

I hesitantly agreed at least to meet the shih-tzu. The mother and daughter were able to get him into the car and brought him to me the next day. The shih-tzu was, without a doubt, extraordinarily cute. He had a little baby-doll face. The fact that he was also only ten pounds made him even more adoptable—as long as no one looked at him, did not get closer than three feet of him, and, most definitely, did not attempt to touch him or feed him. Under any of these circumstances, he wanted to eat his prey for lunch.

"Isn't he adoptable?" the mother and daughter asked in tandem.

This was one of those rare instances in my life where I was speechless.

"You'll be able to work with him, and I'm sure many people will want him," the daughter said.

The mother said, "I really enjoyed having him, but he chases my cats. I would love to keep him. If it wasn't for that, I would."

Staring at her bandaged hands, I asked, "Have either of you been able to touch him or hold him?"

"He sat in my mother's lap on the way home from the shelter when we adopted him," the daughter said. "I would love to have him too, but

Danger in disguise

I just can't. I don't have the time to work with him. We will help you in any way we can if you take him."

Both the mother and daughter took turns praising me, saying, "Randi, you're so good at what you do. He really needs someone like you to help him. We're sure he's had a rough life."

But what I was staring at seemed to be a Tasmanian devil who only stopped baring his teeth when he was ignored. My head said, "No, Randi. There's something abnormally wrong with this dog—don't do it," my heart said, "Well, maybe with some time he'll learn to trust and warm up to people if given the space and training he needs."

So, with the pleading, hopeful faces of this mother-daughter duo staring at me, I allowed my thirteen years of experience to be overruled by my attraction to them. With their promise to support my efforts to work with this dog, the baby-doll-faced Tasmanian devil joined the list of Recycled Pets' available dogs.

After over a week with the shih-tzu, I was still not able to pick him up or touch him without him snarling and biting. When I slowly approached to feed him, squatting down low to be as unthreatening as possible, he would always become angry, growling and baring his teeth. He was content to be alone and happily entertained himself dancing around and playing with toys. He never showed any signs of fear and even began jumping up and greeting me when I returned home. But when I attempted to pet him, he always lunged at me with rage.

My mother, who worked from home to be with the emotionally and physically challenged dogs I had rescued, felt sorry for this little guy, even though he never showed any signs of abuse. She volunteered to let him share her space. I felt comfortable with this because I knew she would respect him, letting him be unless he told her otherwise.

Over the next couple of days, it did appear that he was bonding with her. He began sleeping next to her and dancing around like a puppy to play with her. But still, any eye contact that was made with him would result in his baring his teeth and becoming more hostile. I realized that although he was becoming more comfortable and outgoing, he had not become less aggressive or less unpredictable. This dog was not in any way more adoptable than when he had come to me.

It was usually easy for me to determine the difference between a frightened, insecure dog that is just a bit snappy and that rare one that may have something neurologically wrong with it. It was now becoming very clear to me that this baby-faced shih-tzu seemed to be the latter.

After two weeks, I was in a quandary over what to do with this unstable dog that was taking the spot of other dogs I could have been helping. I phoned the daughter and said, "Help. I don't know what to do with this little guy. He has not shown any improvement, and I haven't been able even to attempt to begin to show him to anyone. Do you think either of you could help out and foster him while I continue to work on advertising and placing him?"

"I'm sorry, Randi, but neither of us can take him. I'm sure he'll be fine. He just needs time," she said. "We both feel we saved his life for a reason. Please let us know how he's doing. We really do care about him."

I was even more speechless than when I had first met this dog.

Several more days had passed when I received a call on my cell phone from my mother, who calmly said, "Randi, come here right away. You need to come get this dog. I have him closed off in the bathroom."

About twenty minutes later I arrived at her house. It looked like a war zone. Blood was splattered on the walls, bed, and floor, and my mother's bloody handprints were on the doorknob of her bathroom.

The shih-tzu had been quietly asleep in the bed next to her as she was reading the paper. He awoke and she noticed that he was staring at her out of the corner of his eyes. My mother knew enough to let him be, but he began growling at her and wouldn't stop. As she slowly moved away from him, not making eye contact and attempting to get out of bed, this ten-pound thing attacked her.

Trying to get him off her, she fell to the ground. Had he not been wearing a collar, she didn't know how she would have been able to dislodge his teeth from her arm. The only way she was able to break his grip was by grabbing his collar through the pool of blood and throwing him into the bathroom, quickly shutting the door behind him.

As I walked through her house, the other dogs appeared as if they had gone through this with her since they had seen the entire battle. They were unusually quiet and seemed unsure as to what they were supposed to do.

I was able to put a crate in the doorway to the bathroom to scoot this dog into it so he would not be running free. I was never able to touch him to pick him up. He was growling most of the time that I drove him back to the vet where the mother and daughter had had him neutered. It was then that the veterinary technician at the animal hospital informed me about the opinion that the vet gave after handling this shih-tzu.

The technician said, "I can't believe they gave this dog away. We also were not able to handle him due to his aggressiveness, and we told them he would be a danger to place. We advised against it. We're so sorry that this happened. Leave him here, and we'll contact them."

I did just that.

Sadly, I received the only angry and degrading letter in my entire rescuing career from the daughter, who stated that animal rescuers owe it to the world to take on cases like this one. According to her, I simply wasn't taking responsibility for my choices, and I should have kept the shih-tzu.

Although my mother has scars and nerve damage from this attack, this experience has not changed her compassionate and forgiving nature. While I searched deep within myself to find a way to make peace with this situation, I remembered my mother's beautiful, soft voice saying, "Randi, these people were only trying to help this dog. He couldn't help the way he was. He had no control over his actions. I still feel sorry for him."

Amazingly, my mother has continued nurturing many of the abandoned and abused dogs that I rescue, even though she remains fearful whenever she hears an occasional "normal" growl.

I honored my mother's strength and resiliency at this time in my life when I seriously began questioning my own. My desire to continue helping the hundreds of people who come to me to relieve them of their pets was now fading into my past. I felt as if I was being buried alive, emotionally, physically, and financially.

A part of me was now praying that this passion could permanently be put to sleep.

CHAPTER 16

ROONEY'S STORY
October 21, 1999

I n every dog lover's life comes that one in a million match that you absolutely know, without a doubt, shares your "DNA." Although you've had other dogs you adore and cherish, this one you know has been with you throughout eternity. This is the one you tell yourself daily your life could not do without.

Rooney, the precocious petit basset-griffon Vendeen mix who entered my life in October 1989, was that one for me. He was the "elf" who made us all laugh and taught us to take life in stride. I was mesmerized by his mischievousness, cuteness, and spirit for the ten brief years I was blessed by his presence. On October 21, 1999, Rooney showed me just how temporary life can be.

I was flying high as one of the top consultants who introduced magnetic health care products to North America. Because of that, I had been able to purchase my first beautiful house less than a month earlier. I hadn't yet moved in but visited often. I was now also driving a magnificent white Jaguar convertible, complements of Nikken, the magnet company, in addition to my 4x4 Rooney-mobile. I often heard many

Rooney in bee suit

comments such as "Randi, why don't you use your Jaguar as a big planter? Since all of your dogs don't fit in it, you never drive it." But I ignored all of that and was so very grateful to have such an incredible masterpiece of a vehicle sitting in my garage to take my own breath away.

As busy as I was, I still seemed to find the time to run my dog rescue agency. And busy I was. So busy I wasn't aware of what I was doing much of the time. So busy I couldn't have possibly been in the moment while concentrating on so many things at the same time. And so busy I thought it was best to leave my impish son, Rooney, alone for the first time with a groomer.

The grooming room where I had left Rooney was in the back of a veterinary clinic. I was showing one of my adoption dogs, Bumblebee Potter, a delicate Shetland-sheepdog mix, to a lady in the front of the clinic. I rescued Bumblebee Potter from the Ventura County animal shelter on her last day of life after I looked into her auburn, soulful eyes. I was close to keeping her myself as she seemed to be overly sensitive and had some issues that most people wouldn't tolerate. She had been debarked and submissively urinated when most people would approach her. She would cry or snap when she was picked up, petted in certain ways, or brushed. But she was so affectionate, smart, loyal, and gorgeous that, to me, Bee Potter was beyond perfect.

This was one of the few rare times in almost ten years that Rooney was out of my sight. But I was also becoming protective over Bee Potter and wouldn't leave her with just anyone until I felt it was safe.

Suddenly, I heard a bloodcurdling scream pulsating from the grooming room—"Randi!" When I ran to see what had happened, the owner of the grooming shop was running through the veterinary clinic carrying Rooney in a towel, shouting, "Get the vets! Get the vets!" Rooney had been left tied in a tub, sitting alone. The groomer had gone home without telling me. The owner of the shop had found Rooney hanging on the outside of the tub from his neck—lifeless.

As I stood at a distance, watching a group of vets and their assistants pour their hearts into bringing Rooney back to life, a hot tingling sensation came over me. My head was on fire. Everything seemed to be going in slow motion, and from a dark, floating fog, I heard the faint echo of voices whispering, "Randi, come over here and pet him. Talk to him. Call out his name. Maybe he'll respond to you." But, for the first time in my life, I was so petrified that my body and vocal cords became immobilized. I shut down with a calmness that represented years of burying my emotions to enable myself to survive all I experienced as a dog rescuer. On October 21, 1999, with the unexpected death of my son, Rooney, came the end of my type A personality.

Cognitively, I believed the soul didn't die. Logically, I was grateful Rooney didn't grow old through pain and suffering. But my soul didn't care what my mind knew. It felt as if it had died with him.

The following months I spent screaming to the universe, "Roooooney! Where are you?" I wanted to believe I heard him screaming for me too.

I spent months driving the coast, writing and begging for this emptiness to be taken away. The world now seemed so meaningless. My beautiful Jaguar and new house now meant nothing to me. All of the things I once cared about that kept me busy were now replaced with feelings of weakness and apathy. I was exhausted from crying so hard for so many months that I couldn't force myself to care about anything since Rooney had been gone.

The last Christmas of the century I spent with my dogs, still missing those special feelings Rooney had given me. Joy was an emotion now entombed deep in my past life.

I spent the turn of the century with two of my closest friends, Mitch and Barbara. Since adopting their dogs, Munchkin and Roxy, from me, they were the only friends with whom I ever wanted to celebrate anything, especially this new year. They were not surprised when I left early to be alone again.

In the new year, I still found myself losing track of time. One misty February night, with my truck backed up on a cliff, overlooking the ocean, I sat on my tailgate for hours. It was very dark and quiet when I thought I saw a car pull up close to me. It sounded as if a small group of people exited the car while talking to each other. The familiar jingle of dog tags made me less annoyed at this invasion of my privacy. About ten minutes later, when they returned to their car and drove away, the sound of the dog tags remained. A ray of hope shot through me when I thought that this dog was really Rooney trying to find his way back to me. But four months void of necessary sleep made me wonder if that entire scenario was real or imagined. There was no dog and perhaps not even a car full of people. I would never be quite sure.

Since Rooney died, I had lost my sense of direction. I completely lost my desire to continue running my rescue. I knew I couldn't handle the responsibility any longer. The effort it took merely to exist was more than I was willing to give. It was that night that I decided to sell my house and Jaguar.

Remembering Rooney in
his jester suit

CHAPTER 17

ROONEY TOO
March 2000

On March 1 of 2000, less than five months after Rooney left me, I numbly and unexpectedly said good-bye to my dachshund, Heidi. I found her floating in the pool where she once played. I was home when it happened, but heard nothing. My heart had no room left to grieve.

For weeks, I had been receiving messages from volunteers about dogs needing to be rescued out of one particular animal shelter in Los Angeles. I had never gone there because it was in a dangerous part of L.A., and the dogs were said to be living in deplorable conditions. Very few rescuers set foot in this shelter due to the expense of bringing the dogs to an adoptable state. Not a place for those with weak stomachs.

But the coaxing of several of my volunteers made it impossible for me to ignore all of the messages about the help that was needed at this shelter.

Linda, one of my newest, cherished foster moms, pleaded with me. "Randi, please, let's go to this shelter. I'll drive and you'll be okay. I promise. You don't have to do anything but come with me and help save some dogs' lives. I'll foster whichever dogs you pick out to rescue."

On the Saturday after Heidi died, I accompanied Linda to the shelter in my close-to-zombie state. When we arrived just before closing time, Linda and I were both in agreement. This was the filthiest, most overcrowded shelter we had ever seen. It was not uncommon to hear many negative and untrue rumors flying about throughout Southern California of certain rescue organizations and animal shelters. But all of the rumors that we had been hearing about this shelter were true. Some of the dogs had fresh wounds from being attacked by each other due to overcrowding. It was the end of the day. The dogs we did not select who were available would be euthanized. We had less than an hour to decide whom we would save.

I had a spectacular home awaiting a well-tempered Tibetan terrier mix or something shaggy of this sort. Many of the dogs at this shelter either were being held for a few days to see if their owners surfaced or had already been adopted and were on hold until being spayed or neutered the following Monday. But there was a brilliant, medium-sized, shaggy Tibetan terrier mix available. He was only minutes away from being destroyed. I suspected that this sweet boy was not adopted because one side of his neck had been shaved and had a large drain protruding out of it. He was very innocent and did not stand up to the other dogs in his run who apparently ganged up on him.

"Linda," I said, "this one is a definite. Let's do the paper work for him and get out of here. I'll have another volunteer pick him up at the vet after he's neutered Monday. Come on. Let's go."

"But, Randi," Linda very gently and sweetly pleaded with me, "I really want to help anyone else we can take. I really miss fostering the dogs. I don't mind taking one or two more."

"I'm tired," I apathetically said, "Let's go home."

As we were walking out to the office to do the paper work, we stopped at one of the runs jammed with smaller dogs.

"God! How many dogs can they cram in there? How can this even be legal?" I preached to Linda, who knew better than to listen to my complaints. "They're all so matted and sickly looking. Thank God they've all been adopted by the looks of what's written on their kennel cards. It's a good thing they'll all be fixed Monday and off to their new homes."

Then I noticed that one card did not fit in. "Hey, Linda! Look at this kennel card that says an available female Staffordshire terrier is in this cage! This is a male cage and I sure don't see any Staffordshire terriers mixed in with these little guys. Let's get a kennel worker."

I was now invigorated with the thought of correcting an error, possibly resulting in a dog's life being saved. I ran off to find any available kennel worker before the shelter closed, while Linda stayed by the dog run.

I returned with a young girl who was wearing an animal control uniform. She didn't look old enough to be working anywhere and acted as if we were doing nothing more than wasting her time. She seemed to be quite annoyed with the extra work we were now giving her.

Linda very politely asked, "Would you mind helping us figure out which dog goes to this kennel card? We know you're closing, but we wouldn't want it to be put to sleep if we can take it. We have a dog rescue."

"I don't know," the young girl said. "Figure it out and come back and get me. I have to finish cleanin' the runs."

"We can't figure out which dog belongs to this card. This is why I came to get you in the first place," I said. "It doesn't look like there's a female Staffordshire terrier in this cage."

The kennel worker shrugged and left. I went through all of the kennel cards with Linda, matching each dog with its appropriate card. We finally narrowed it down to one small dog that was nearly bald and without a card to match it's description.

I took the card that read "female Staffordshire terrier" back to the kennel worker, who was hosing down some of the dog runs across from us. She shook her head at me as though I was bothering her once again, but she did take the card.

She quickly glanced at all of the kennel cards, went into the dog run, and pointed to the nearly bald dog. "It looks like it's this one. But I ain't touchin' it. It's listed here as a biter."

"That's not a Staffordshire terrier," I said. "It's about five times too small, and this is a male dog cage. That card says 'female' on it."

"I don't know," the young kennel worker said. "I gotta go. We're closin'. You gotta leave now."

With an undisguised look of disgust, I turned to Linda and said, "What should we do?"

Linda sweetly said, "Maybe she'll let us hold him or her."

"I don't know, Linda," I said. "That dog looks pretty rancid. It's a scabby mess with sparse patches of dreadlocks, and it's pretty dumpy and pathetic looking. It's going to be a project to clean up and get adopted, and it's listed as a biter. Let's just go home."

Linda jumped in and said, "I'll take it!"

This was so Linda-ish. She was always willing to foster anything. She was one of the most unconditionally loving people I had ever known when it came to dogs. Linda worked very long hours as the director of a prestigious company and was still always bubbly and more than willing to drive any distance or go without sleep to help a dog.

With a smile on my face, I went back to the kennel worker and ever so sweetly asked, "Do you think you would let me attempt to handle that little dog? I don't mind if it bites me. I will sign a release if you want."

Over a decade of rescuing dogs had taught me how to sweetly ask people for help when they may have preferred to do otherwise. This was a tough lesson for me; more often than not, I really wanted to act the opposite. But I had learned to focus on my goal at any given time and bypass my ego. In an effort to reach the goal that now stood before me—possibly saving this dog's life—I began praising the young kennel worker.

"Thank you so much," I said, "for all of your hard work here and for helping us figure out what the story is with this little dog. If you would be so brave as to get it out of the cage for us, we would be forever grateful to you."

It's amazing how well this often works. The kennel worker instantly smiled as she went into the cage of the "biting female Staffordshire terrier," with a herd of other small dogs jumping up on her.

"I'm afraid to pick it up," she said.

I noticed that it was calmly sitting in the back of the cage with its curly, bald tail drumming against the wall, and I said, "I don't know. It looks pretty harmless to me. Maybe you could slip your leash around its neck and see how it reacts."

She did, and the "biting female Staffordshire terrier" did nothing.

I then asked, "Do you think you could try to carefully pick it up so we could see if it's a boy or a girl?"

"I don't know," she said. "This card says this dog's been bitin'. I don't wanna risk it."

"Well, why don't you give it a shot? It looks like you really know what you're doing. You can get away quickly enough if it does try to bite you."

The entire time I was really thinking: This process could have been over in seconds if she had just let me into this dog run. But before I knew it, the little dog was in her arms, and she was petting it.

"Is it a boy or a girl?" I asked.

She flipped the dog onto its back. It went completely limp, as though it either had no cartilage in its body—or had died.

"Oh God, is it okay?" I asked. "Can you feel a pulse? Check its gums."

"I ain't stickin' my hands in this dog's mouth. It's alive, and it still could bite me."

"Well, either that's a little dreadlock tangled with the others on its underside, or it's a boy. It seems pretty mellow. Why don't you see if you can lift up his lips so we can look at his teeth and guess his approximate age?"

I turned to Linda who was intently watching and whispered, "If this homely thing is really old, we're not taking him. He's already going to be quite a project, and if he's old, he'll never get adopted."

The kennel worker sighed, but went ahead and lifted the lip of this smelly, scabby little dog. While playing dead, he passed all of the tests. He didn't try to bite, and he looked to be under ten years old.

"Okay," I said to the kennel worker, "we'll take this one too. But where is his kennel card?"

"This is it!" she said, as she handed me the card that read *Staffordshire Terrier-female-biter.* "You have to leave now. We're closed. You can pick up your dogs Monday at the vet, after they're neutered."

Linda came with me to the office where I completed the paper work to adopt the two dogs. We drove home still baffled about the biting female Staffordshire terrier.

By the time Monday rolled around, my apathy had returned, and I again had no desire to put any effort into these new rescues. But when Julie Prem, another volunteer, pulled into my driveway, excitedly smiling and waving at me even after battling Los Angeles rush-hour traffic, I had to attempt to reciprocate some of her enthusiasm. Julie had the two new rescues in the backseat of her car and, after picking them up from the vet, was already falling in love.

She rolled down her window, put her finger up to her mouth, and quietly said, "Shhhh—they're still asleep from the anesthesia from being neutered. They're both so cute aren't they?"

I peeked my head in quickly. "These aren't our dogs! Who gave you these dogs?"

"The receptionist at the vet's office," she said.

"Oh my God! They gave you the wrong dogs. We have someone else's dogs," I said.

"How was I supposed to know?" Julie defended herself. "I never even saw them."

"No, it's not your fault, Julie. The vet's office or shelter made a mistake. I'll call them."

Julie continued to blame herself and said, "I feel so bad. I should have known. But look at how cute this one is. Even though he's asleep his tail wagged the entire time we were driving."

I took a closer look and gasped. "Oh God! That's the right dog, the homely one. Why couldn't they have switched that one by mistake? The other one we took out of the shelter has someone waiting to adopt him from me. Where could he be? Maybe we can return this homely one to the vet and they won't know the difference. That other one next to him looks like a pure Maltese. We should try to keep him. We'll place him in an instant."

Julie looked up at me and said, "Randi, we can't do that. I'll call the vet so we can figure this out."

"I know," I said. "I was only joking, but it was a fleeting thought."

When Julie phoned the vet, indeed there was a hysterical woman at the front desk wanting to know where her precious, purebred Maltese was. Although our homely "project" wasn't much bigger than a Maltese, I suspect, if we had attempted to switch the dogs, the owner would have quickly figured out that mistake. I was told that when the vet gave this woman our twenty-five-pound Tibetan terrier mix with a shaved neck and a drain protruding out of it, she almost fainted.

Although none of this was Julie's fault, she felt so horrible about the mix-up that she volunteered to spend most of the following day driving dogs to their proper destinations. I, on the other hand, wanted to move to the coast of Maine to get away from all of this. But instead, I ended up keeping these two dogs at my house for the night because Julie was off to work and the vet's office was now closed.

The Maltese went back to its owner the next day. The other dog we had rescued, the Tibetan terrier mix, was returned to us and adopted that same day by the lady who was eagerly awaiting his arrival.

Meanwhile, I couldn't bear to see the homely, unadoptable project suffer in his filth and scabs with his toenails growing into his skin. I immediately groomed him and what little fur he had. My obsessiveness seemed to be slowly returning. Actually, I don't think he was suffering as much as I was, smelling him and looking at him, because his tail still hadn't slept and his supposed biting problem seemed to have transformed into a kissing problem. After grooming him, I came to the conclusion that he was either sick, stoned, or had one of the easiest, most placid temperaments that I had seen in thirteen years of rescuing thousands of dogs. He turned out to be snow white and weighed a little over ten pounds. To me, he looked so cute that I put a fancy sweater on him to cover his scabby, bald patches and soon began to show him to prospective parents. He now became *my* project.

Person after person eagerly came to meet my project, ready to adopt him, based on my description: *Immediately goes limp playing dead in anyone's arms like a baby; fetches a ball like a retriever; smarter than most humans; loves other dogs; precociously unboring and the perfect portable size.* He loved causing trouble by doing such things as decorating the house with rolls of toilet paper. He even cajoled the other dogs into joining him in these festivities!

To me, he was everything anyone would ever want in a dog. I couldn't understand why people would spend hours with him, then phone the next day to say they wanted to continue looking for another dog. My own dogs tolerated him as if he had always been with them. He playfully but respectfully forced himself on everyone, giving them no choice but to accept him.

The following month of April, shy Goose, who quickly became one of my mother's most beloved children when he came to us in 1991, unexpectedly became ill. A misdiagnosis by a new vet I had just started using resulted in Goose needing four blood transfusions. In an attempt to save his life, another one of our newer four-legged family members, Buck, donated his blood to Goose. But I had to play God and release

Goose from this planet only three days later. I began to feel again but not in the ways I wanted. Goose had been safe in our care, where he learned to trust humans and shed many of his fears. Releasing him from our protection killed what little part of my heart was left. How could Fate now take my most precious birthday gift from 1991 and end his life in such a painfully brutal way? It seemed as if Fate was planning on taking all of my four-legged loved ones. I was now in a battle with my heart to stop it from feeling anything. My mother went into denial over his unacceptable death.

As I continued to reflect back on the end of Rooney, Heidi, and Goose's lives, I believed the concept of accepting everything as being in Divine Right Order would forever elude me. Would I spend the rest of my life in anger, fearing that everything I loved would be taken from me, afraid to trust, care, and love again?

But as angry as I was at Fate for what it had done to the most important things in my life, it was also Fate that kept bringing my mind forward to the present.

Two weeks after Heidi's tragic death, before Goose left us, I had spoken these words: "If another one of my dogs leaves, my little white project is staying." Could my maternal instincts have known what lurked ahead?

When Goose became ill, my homely project, who had only been here weeks, spent most of his time by his side, gently bathing him in kisses. It was also about this time when I began to notice some mysterious and unearthly things about him. One day, when he was sitting up in my lap while I was putting a sweater on his bald, scabby body, I looked deep into his eyes. When he stared back at me with his tail wagging and then nipped at my nose, that hot, tingling sensation I felt on October 21, 1999, the day Rooney died, crept back up my spine once again. My little white project began resembling *everything* for which my heart felt as though it had stopped beating six months earlier: strutting off to attack men, sitting up to beg while punching me in the face, and imitating Houdini as a skilled escape artist.

My dream came true! Fate brought Rooney back to me in the form of my homely little white project. I named him Rooney Too.

Rooney Too, the ultimate Recycled Pet—
from bald female Staffordshire terrier,
to heavenly Houdini hunk!

CHAPTER 18

THE RESURRECTIONS OF
SKOOTER-BOO 200 IQ
May 5, 2007

"No, no," I cried out while staring over Puget Sound from my deck. My body was trembling, heart racing in horror. The one dog that had stayed with me longer than any had just died in my arms at the age of twenty.

Skooter's entrance into my heart came at the beginning of my life of rescue. Perhaps the most symbolic of the thousands over the years, he would always be the one that represented my Skippy coming back to me—almost like a resurrection. The similarities were not to be questioned if anyone had even an inkling of faith within them. Both scraggly, tan, Benji-type terrier mixes, this style of dog became my claim to rescue fame in the late 1980s, otherwise known as "Randi dogs."

Skooter's ride on Earth was a bumpy one from the start. A concussion from being hit by a car as a stray adult in 1988 landed him in the West Valley Animal Shelter, where I first locked eyes with him. Sitting in the same cage that Skippy had been in five years earlier, after being hit by a car on the same street that almost ended Skippy's life at fourteen, was one of my first introductions to the concept of Divine Right Order. As he was withdrawn, depressed, and not responding to medical treatment, the vets at the shelter were ready to euthanize Skooter. I never knew how tenacious I truly was until Skooter came to me. I won the battle with the vets, and in September of 1988, I brought home the one dog that would teach me more about life, resiliency, and death than any in the nineteen years he spent with me.

It didn't take long to discover that Skooter's apparent depression was anything but that. He was a serious philosopher, who was always in deep thought. Anyone he let into his realm would quickly understand that his IQ exceeded that of most humans. Hence, his full name soon became Skooter-Boo 200 IQ. This was nothing to laugh about. His depression was, in actuality, his concern over the way most everyone conducted their lives. Nineteen event-filled years with him would teach me that we humans are far too dramatic to reason properly, impairing our rational judgment and ability to peacefully maintain control over our decision-making processes. Skooter would be the greatest mentor I would ever know.

Being hit by a car, resulting in a concussion and abrasions over his entire body, quickly became a forgettable part of Skooter's past. I, on the other hand, would begin a nineteen-year worry session, running him to vets, specialists, healers, and psychics. Had I known then what I do today, I would have put some of that time and energy into working on my own neuroses and tuning into Skooter's thoughts.

What often looked like a suffering, depressed soul was instead Skooter's disgust over the immaturity of all of the dogs constantly surrounding him. In addition, I thought Skooter was having aftereffects from his concussion. But he dispelled that concern by silently sharing his truth with me, letting me know that it was my endless babbling that was giving him headaches. Skooter needed a calm and quiet environment so that he could carry on with his philosophizing and meditations. Ending up with me and my unshakable addiction to rescuing dogs was his biggest nightmare.

Skooter had requested a condominium of his own, but I was so engrossed with other, more demanding dogs that I ignored his needs. It was at this time that his voice came to life, which was a squeaky high-pitched one that always spewed out as many intelligent three- to five-syllable words as possible. His IQ continued to expand, and he realized that, if he developed chronic stomach problems, it would get him out of the house and give him the alone time at specialists that he was craving.

After running hundreds of dollars of tests, the first specialist said that Skooter had endocrine problems and would need to be on steroids for the rest of his life or else he would not make it past the age of ten. Skooter's response? "That's ridiculous! Who would be dumb enough to buy into that concept? Let's get out of here!" I agreed, and we had a heart-to-heart talk on the way home. He 'fessed up to acting sick only to get away from the other dogs. I wasn't in the position to buy him his own condo, but I did agree to give him his own room where no other dogs, except for those he invited in, could bother him.

It seemed like an easy resolution, but in the back of my mind I would always wonder if there was some validity to the specialist's prognosis. Skooter never gave it a second thought.

The years seemed to fly by so fast that I hardly realized that Skooter had now entered his preteens and was still here, even without steroids. The specialist was wrong. Skooter's IQ had more wisdom attached to it than all of the impressive training of the specialist. But a routine exam and ultrasound performed by another specialist wrote Skooter off once again: A heart condition would take his life in approximately six months, and there was nothing that could be done for it. I questioned this specialist, "Why can't we just do a heart transplant?" That conversation ended almost as abruptly as I finished the question, with the specialist saying, "No playing, running, hiking, or any other activity for him."

Not a day went by where I did not worry about losing my philosopher. I watched him like a hawk, even though I knew that limiting his activities would not be an issue. Skooter preferred calmly observing his environment. Rarely did he participate in outdoor sports.

Another year had passed, and Skooter was still here. Another specialist was wrong. But I noticed a mass that was growing on one of Skooter's legs faster than any that I had ever seen. This time we opted not to waste more energy with specialists and went to my regular vets at Tarzana Pet Clinic. Skooter had developed a mast cell cancerous tumor that had to be removed as soon as possible because of how quickly it was growing. Surgery was always a risk, especially for heart patients who were supposed to have already died. But Dr. Debbie Hoffman and her new associate, Dr. Gayle Grasmehr, knew Skooter well and had been dealing with my neuroses for over a decade now. They knew that killing Skooter under anesthesia was not an option. But still, not a minute went by before the surgery where I did not feel impending doom. The day before the surgery, I took Skooter alone to the beach in Malibu to run and hike, and on the way home, I celebrated his life by getting him a big hamburger. If that was his last day here, I needed to make it a memorable one.

But once again, my fearful thinking was wrong. Although the vets had to cut into the muscle of Skooter's rear leg to remove all of the cancer, the surgery didn't faze him. The following day he resumed his meditating and carried on as though nothing had happened. Skooter took Tagamet and Benadryl for after-care to ensure that the cancer would not return.

Six years later, Skooter was still with me. Cancer-free, heart attack-free, and steroid-free. All of the negative realities that are an everyday part of the way of the world didn't affect my philosopher. Again, the years had flown by, and I was too consumed by other things to realize that he was, perhaps, no longer a young dog. Skooter had never acted like a young dog anyway, and clearly he always had more maturity and wisdom than the most brilliant of humans. He never bought into others' belief systems. He didn't even allow my eighteen years of worrying about him to impact his psyche or quality of life. But this time, I was sure it was the end for him. He seemed to be in pain, could barely walk, and had blood in his urine. I rushed him to my emergency vet, and the grim news was one I could not walk away from peacefully. Skooter's kidneys and bladder were full of pus and bacteria and were failing. We put him on an intensive course of antibiotics, and I administered subcutaneous fluids in him every day. Two weeks later, when he was rechecked, the grim way of the world was wrong. Skooter's kidneys had, at the age of nineteen, bounced back to normalcy. The gaping eye ulcers he had now developed didn't seem to bother him either. But for me, not a day went by that I didn't feel heart palpitations, worrying about my Skooter. His serious, contemplative, Buddha-like nature was always mistaken by everyone, even me, as suffering. In reality, he was one of the most peaceful, content beings on earth.

September of 2006 was here, and I had been recently drawn to fulfill another dream—spending time in the great Pacific Northwest. I had hoped to start a new, quiet, dog-free life away from everything I knew. Seemingly endless nights at emergency vets and seventy-two-hour marathons won with dogs staring at death's door had taken a toll on me both physically and emotionally. I needed a break from my hectic life. Part of that dream came true. On the week of my forty-fourth birthday, I packed up my truck with as much from my past life as possible. Accompanying me were Rooney, Bumblebee, Hazel, and my Skooter-Boo 200 IQ.

"Are you crazy, Randi?" "You can't just pick up and leave everything you know." "What will your mom do without you?" "Skooter will never make the trip. Be prepared to let him go, knowing this will be your last time together. He's too old for you to put him through that." "You haven't even planned this trip."...

Both Skooter and I ignored the many comments coming from people's negative, limiting belief systems. Finally his presence in my life had conditioned me to ignore the way of the world. With no map, no plans, and no sleep, I shut off my cell phone and got onto the I-5 freeway. Even though we had to stop every few hours so that I could give Skooter the four different eye drops he was now needing and finish off the course of antibiotics for his kidneys and bladder, Skooter was the only one who was eager to explore all of the different rest stops, have a drink of water, and eat. The others had no desire to come out of the truck. They were too nervous to eat, drink, or go to the bathroom. As always, Skooter was the sensible, easy one of the bunch.

Forty hours later, we found nirvana and arrived in the great Pacific Northwest, where our new life awaited us. I was exhausted, delirious, and desperate for sleep.

The following morning at 7 a.m., Skooter woke me up, eager to explore while the others slept. The day seemed to rush by almost as quickly as the eighteen years I had spent with Skooter. With neighbors visiting, my unpacking, and deliveries arriving, I wasn't aware that Skooter was missing. I thought he was asleep with the others, but he was nowhere to be seen. The most quiet, wise, and calm dog ever to share my life had vanished.

We were surrounded by water, cliffs, and wilderness that nurtured eagles, deer, raccoons, and other animals. The likelihood of a nineteen-year-old, nearly blind dog surviving in this new environment on his own infused the negativity of the way of the world back into me.

Just before sundown, a neighbor spotted Skooter in the middle of a fifty-foot vertical cliff by my house. When Skooter saw me, I could hear him quietly start to moan. It appeared that he was conscious. I was determined to get to him even if I lost my own life doing so. I was frantic and attempted to climb the cliff, but it was so steep and covered in brush and thorns that climbing it was impossible. With my legs torn and bloodied, I called 911 from my cell phone and was barely able to talk through my sobbing. Shortly after, two fire and rescue trucks arrived with five men. It took them about forty-five minutes to recover Skooter by dropping a firefighter down the cliff. When I made it to the top of the cliff, where Skooter would be returned to me, the sun was already down. The floodlights that were set up were illuminating what looked like a halo of a dog walking away from the rescue site toward my house. It was Skooter, walking away without a scratch on him while I stared in disbelief, with blood running down my legs.

Skooter couldn't be bothered with all of the drama and came into the house ready for dinner. Rooney, Bumblebee, and Hazel were not hungry and fell asleep. It was as though a pair of invisible arms had formed around Skooter, cushioning him down the cliff that should have been his last death sentence.

At nineteen, Skooter finally became my priority. With a constant stream of thousands of other dogs needing my attention over the years, Skooter, with his quiet, undemanding nature, was always the forgotten middle child. He rarely wanted any attention, was angered by anyone treating him like a baby or a dog, and usually preferred to be alone. Now that his body was becoming a tad bit fragile and he had dodged the doors of Death numerous times, I would finally take advantage of truly bonding with the one dog who had been with me longer than any.

Skooter rejoiced in our new-found relationship. He loved the cooler weather, rain, and experiencing snow for the first time. His body seemed to be getting stronger after the age of nineteen than it had been in years. His temperament was shifting too. He now wanted to be close to me, making sure I was within his sight when he was not sleeping. The independent philosopher was now allowing me to baby him for the first time in his life. He would nestle into my arms, pressing his head against

my face, when I held him upside down, kissing his velveteen ears. Both
of us were in ecstasy over our new relationship, and Skooter became my
new puppy.

I ordered an all-terrain dog stroller so that I could take the entire
clan to the hiking trails that are within walking distance from our house.
I was hoping to push both Skooter and Rooney together in the stroller,
but Skooter would have nothing of it. He wanted to ride alone. So
Rooney, who refuses to walk on a leash and wants to be held constantly,
ended up in a baby-sling style carrier around my neck. Bumblebee and
Hazel escorted us by leash on either side of the stroller, and this turned
into some of the greatest cardiovascular activity I had ever known. By
the time we made it through the hills to the hiking trails, Bumblebee
and Hazel were ready to collapse, and Skooter was usually angry with
me for taking away his control. He welcomed the release of his frustra-
tions on the hiking trails and would growl at me as I lifted him out of
the stroller. He was always eager to escape the stroller bondage that I had
forced upon him and would often lead us on the trails. When our hikes
were over, Skooter would again become angry. Slowly and deliberately,
he would attempt to sneak off and go for a second round of hiking, leaving the rest of us behind. His preference to be alone had never left him.
His love of hiking only came after the age of nineteen.

The year 2007 was here, and I was finally realizing that my anxiety
over losing Skooter, due to some illusion of an illness, was vanishing. He
was now twenty and enjoying his new life as much as I was. Skooter had
taken on my night-owl hours and was usually the only one up with me
until the sun rose. His appetite was the best at around 4 a.m., so I made
it a point to stay up at least until that time to feed him. He was aware
of how important it was to chew each bite of food very slowly and thoroughly, and if I did not sit with him, sometimes he would forget he was
eating and fall asleep with his head in his bowl. I never thought he ate
enough, so my neuroses led me to attempt to feed him as many times as
possible so that he would not waste away. Needless to say, hours of my
days and nights were spent feeding Skooter.

My body had always required only a few hours of sleep in a twenty-
four- to forty-eight-hour period. It took me eight months to realize that
when Skooter slept until early evening, he was not suffering or deathly
ill. We had been up together all night, eating, pacing along our deck

An evening stroll

overlooking the water, and contemplating the mysteries of all that exists in the universe.

It was now May the fifth. This was a sacred time for me. Hazel, one of my unadoptables who accompanied me on this life change, had a birthday the previous day. Hazel had come to me years ago and was one of the most tortured souls I had ever rescued. She had been severely abused in ways that most people would find incomprehensible. Her owners went to jail, but that didn't heal her body or spirit. She was a female replica of Buster, a concoction of different breeds—both long, low, big-headed, shaggy, and with painfully damaged souls. Although the people who brought Hazel to me said that she was a sweet, pure-bred Lhasa apso and failed to tell me anything about her abuse or temperament, when I saw her I knew that Buster had sent her to me. As cute as Hazel was, though, no one would commit to adopting her because she could not trust enough to look anyone in the eyes, show affection, or bond. The first six months she spent with me, she either was hiding under the bed or was on my mom's kitchen table, away from the other dogs, just as Buster had done. To me, there was not a more perfect dog on Earth. I let Hazel be herself and growl at me as much as she needed to. It took me a year to understand that I could kiss her as much as I wanted, with her growling at me, and she would not bite. I ignored the many comments from outsiders: "This dog is a lawsuit waiting to happen." "You cannot place her, and if you do keep her, you'll lose your house after she attacks someone and they sue you." "I know you think she has a great temperament, Randi, but she's a time-bomb that can go off at any minute." "She needs to be put to sleep."

Depression and negativity aren't allowed to thrive for long in my environment, and Hazel slowly learned that with me, whatever she needed to do would never be judged. But just at the time she began to trust, she developed cancer throughout her mammary glands. Skooter talked her through it. "It's no big deal. Everyone around you will try to make it seem as if it's the end of the world, but don't believe them. The vets will knock you out, and Randi will bring you home the minute you're up from the anesthesia—even if it's in the middle of the night. It's just residual stuff from your past life, and you'll never have to think about it again."

Skooter-Boo 200 IQ

Nineteen-year-old Skooter hiking
in his first winter snow

Hazel took Skooter's advice and overcame it just the way Skooter did with these minor bumps in the road.

After that, Hazel took a liking to Skooter. He was the first dog she showed affection toward, and I would catch the two of them off on their own, flirting with one another in the backyard.

Hazel's birthday happens to be two days before my mom's birthday. Hazel seemed to take a liking to her too. The two of them were like twins, and Hazel preferred to dine on my mom's bed with her, away from the other dogs. They spent their nights together in bed, watching TV and ignoring each other. Hazel prefers not to be touched, but likes to stare at people. This drove my mom crazy, and she would repeatedly say, "It's not fair. If I'm not allowed to touch her, she's not allowed to be that cute." Watching those two bond and finally seeing Hazel dance reminded me that my life has served a purpose.

This was the first birthday weekend of my mom's where I was not with her in California, but she preferred not to be bothered by humans anyway, particularly me and the clan of dogs that were a part of the package. She had confiscated Marvin and Ernest from me, two little teenage, diabetic unadoptables, and they were more than enough for her to handle. We became better friends than ever since I left California, and I coached her, via telephone, on how to care for Marvin and Ernest.

So this May was a notable one. I had hoped to spend those few days writing and enjoying my new view of life. I let Skooter sleep all day and didn't bother him once. He finally awoke in the early evening and was hungry, so I fed him and gave the others some snacks. I was about to climb into bed to sleep a little, but Skooter now needed to go out. We went out on the deck, and he had one of his most healthy bowel movements ever, which always makes me happy. "Good boy! That's just the way I like to see them," I commented to him.

He wasn't entirely awake yet and slowly came stumbling into the house, bumping into the sofas. I picked Skooter up and took him back out on the deck so that he could also urinate before we took a nap. His rear legs went out from under him, which wasn't uncommon. I picked him up again and gently put him back down. He fell over on his side and could not stand. I again picked him up and just held him close. He then stretched up his head and yelped out a high-pitched cry several times. His head dropped down, tongue fell out, and body went limp. In the blink of an eye, Skooter had just dropped dead in my arms.

I held him even tighter. When I realized that he was gone, I quietly cried out, "No, no." I wasn't ready for this day. I had done nothing to prepare for it. I continued to hold his limp body and was also now supporting his head. I was trembling, my mouth went dry and my heart was palpitating. This day was never supposed to come. I didn't want to let go of him, but after several minutes, I gently laid his body down on the deck.

I thought about breathing into his mouth to bring him back. But I checked his gums, which were already stark white. I felt his heart, which was no longer beating. Then I cupped my hand over his bumpy, round head, as I had craved to do nineteen years earlier, the day I had first laid eyes on him as a stray at the shelter. He was already cold. I then watched as his body released the last remaining life left in him through his urine.

Those few moments felt like forever. Skooter exited the earth plane with the same style, wisdom, and grace in which he had lived his entire life—easily and as free of drama as possible.

It was the end of an era. My rescue began out of the unbearable pain I had experienced when I had lost my childhood dog Skippy in my early twenties. Skooter had always represented Skippy coming back to me. He was an identical twin of the first dog I had ever loved. Skooter became the forgotten middle child when my life became entwined with thousands of other more demanding dogs, just as Lucky and Skippy had been forgotten as I entered my preteen years and became obsessed with playing the flute. I was given a chance to redeem myself when Skippy was hit by a car at fourteen, just as I was by giving Skooter a new life at the age of nineteen. But still—this day was never supposed to happen. My new relationship with Skooter had only just begun.

It was now dark, and I was not going to leave Skooter's body outside on my deck. I was still trembling uncontrollably. As I carried his body into the house to lay him on his dog bed in the living room, I realized that I had forgotten how to breathe. Or maybe I just didn't care to any longer.

Bizarrely, the other dogs were paying no attention to any of this. Perhaps they finally had absorbed some of Skooter's wisdom, allowing us to have this last time alone together.

No vets were open near me, and the closest emergency vets were over an hour away. Even though Skooter had been gone for what felt like forever, my engrained response was not to give up. I went into my bedroom to get my healing chi machine and was thinking of covering his body with a magnetic blanket.

When I rushed back into the living room, had I not been conscious enough to start breathing properly and stay composed, I would have definitely passed out. There was Skooter, ignoring me and calmly eating an old cookie that had been left on the very dog bed, where I just placed his lifeless body. I could hear his thoughts more clearly than ever before. "What? More drama? I never did buy into the way of the world. Did you really think I would start now? Haven't you learned anything from me yet?"

Four days later we were back on the hiking trails. Skooter dictated his life story to me while on a forty-five-minute hike. Although he is rapidly approaching drinking age this year, twenty-one, he chooses to abstain from bars and alcohol. He also chooses to abstain from steroids, heart conditions, cancer, and death.

Through much of Skooter's life, I found myself having anxiety over some proposed illness with which he had been labeled, fearing it to be the only truth. Skooter has proved that we can create any reality that suits us best—not limit ourselves to the ones others put on us. Skooter remains my greatest mentor.

My journey through Recycled Pets has taught me that everything clearly is in Divine Right Order, no matter how life may appear. For the sake of those whose lives depend on our mercy, we must remove limiting, fear-based beliefs to allow the impossible to transform into the possible.

Today my other passion is in connecting with healers and healing modalities that defy the grim illusions of conventional medicine and thinking. By removing limiting beliefs and focusing only on our dreams and goals, I have discovered that we have the power to manifest anything—even bringing back energies that we felt our life could not do without.

The infinite miracles that I have been blessed to experience consistently boggle the minds of people and veterinarians worldwide. And today, on the twenty-year anniversary of starting my rescue, I invite you to join me in adopting this faith and embracing the miracles that are waiting to be claimed by us all: unleash your belief systems, shine your own unique light on the world, and begin celebrating a life where the impossible becomes possible.

Fabulous family photo

EPILOGUE

What motivates one to devote his or her life to helping animals' lives? Passion? A meaningful purpose? Boredom? Insanity?

It usually starts with helping one or two. If rescuing is in your blood, the rush of bringing peace and safety to God's innocent four-legged children will become the basis of a newfound honorable addiction. And for the numerous people who say "I envy you. I would love to do what you do," I say, "Live the life of an obsessive-compulsive rescuer for just a few days, and then reevaluate that envy."

It can and will become all-consuming. Your life is at the mercy of that 3 a.m. call from a distraught person—"I don't know what to do. A stray shepherd has crawled under my car and is giving birth to puppies. The rain is coming down so hard, and they must be wet and freezing. The mother won't let me get near them, and I think some of the puppies have already died." Or that terrified terrier, running on the freeway in rush-hour traffic when you're on the way to the airport. Or that shell-shocked shih-tzu, whose eye ruptures on New Year's Eve. Or the dachshund who injures her back as you're leaving for your best friend's wedding. Or that unadoptable, thirteen-year-old, cloudy-eyed cockapoo, trembling in the corner of the shelter he was just turned into because his owner died before he did. Most animal lovers can't stay around this for long.

Of the thirty to fifty calls I often received on a daily basis, many were from people giving up their dogs for a variety of reasons, some justified and many simply out of thoughtlessness. Over seventy-five percent were people giving up their pets that were between five and fifteen years old. How many of you are interested in adopting a blind, snappy, fourteen-year-old Lhasa apso? This owner hoped that someone else would want to take on the pleasure of his once-cherished four-legged child, who, due to age, is now incontinent. How about the many people who give up their dogs because they choose to travel or to move to a "no pets" facility rather than follow through on the last few years of commitment to the most loyal friend they ever had?

And so, year after year, when anger returned and often consumed my life, I learned how critical it was to keep myself consciously centered and stay focused on my goals. My immense gratitude goes to those who have helped me reach my goals with my rescue efforts: the shelter workers who bent the rules to save dogs on death row, the foster parents who loved and let go, the veterinarians who donated their services, the volunteers who held the dogs on adoption days, and the hundreds of people who empowered me with their support and encouragement over the years when the tribulations seemed insurmountable.

While cruising down Ventura Boulevard through the San Fernando Valley, now my home away from home but still as familiar to me as my reflection in the mirror, my mind once again takes me back to the beginning. The angry, determined little girl with the long red braids found her place on this planet. Many of the pet shops that were graced by the tender spirits of thousands of unwanted dogs I had rescued and shown at my open house adoptions have now been replaced by other businesses. Condominiums now sit where voices from beyond once spoke to the child in me from the sacred Indian burial grounds. Many of the volunteers who so graciously spent their days helping me run my adoptions have gone off to start their own rescue agencies. I remember all of their smiles as if I saw them yesterday.

My first twenty years of Recycled Pets was a microcosm of all that exists—birth and death, tears and laughter, disagreements and forgiveness, poverty and richness, pain and healing, anger and peace, exhaustion and vitality, loneliness and fulfillment, hopelessness and faith.

As I turn down White Oak Avenue in my Rooney-proof Bronco— now a faded shade of green with rattles and creaks and scratched windows graffitied by dogs' toenails—the sun beams down upon a familiar woman slowly walking two dogs. A tear gently caresses my cheek as I realize that this gray-muzzled, wobbly-legged brother and sister were adopted from me as puppies over a decade ago. It's a gentle reminder of what has kept me going through most of my adult life.

Our four-legged companions are here to teach us to remove any blocks to loving and feeling more passionately and unconditionally than we ever thought possible. Then, always too soon, they are gone.

Most of the stars within these pages have shed their earthly packages, with their humans by their side. They were the lucky ones. If these words have opened one human's heart to find room for just one more "recycled pet," they have served their purpose. If they have helped just one person understand the limitless miracles that are possible here, then I have triumphed.

The morning I finished my first draft of this book, March 29, 2002, which was Good Friday, Buck, who was Goose's blood donor, unexpectedly transcended in the arms of my mother. As had happened when Skippy had died fifteen years earlier, all of the electricity went out in the house. It was yet another message from beyond, reminding me of the unexplainable and incredible powers that dogs radiate throughout our world. When Buck slipped away, my mother didn't even realize that she had fractured her back during the two hours she spent trying to save him. Numb to her own body, she said that the peacefulness in Buck's eyes let her know he wasn't suffering the way she was over losing him. While driving to her house, engulfed by fear and sorrow, these soothing words came to me:

"Transcending from earth is merely the rest between two beats in a grand symphony. But for those four-legged ones that have moved on, you leave behind a longing for your physical presence that will never die in the heart of a dog addict. May every being know only bliss when he transcends."

In honor and memory of each of you with whom I was blessed to share a brief moment in time.

'Til we all meet again.

Heidi and Buck together again

Recycled Pets' Contact Information

P.O. Box 260204
Encino, CA 91426
www.recycledpetsrescue.com
Email: info@recycledpetsrescue.com